ÉGLISE GNOSTIQUE

HISTORY, SACRAMENTS AND TEACHINGS

JULES DOINEL

&

RUNE ØDEGAARD

KRYSTIANIA

Église Gnostique. History, Sacraments and
Teachings
© Rune Ødegaard 2017

Krystiania
Oslo, Norway

First edition 2017

Cover: Sølvi Nykland

Set with 12/20 pt. Arno Pro
Paper: 70 g Crawford Opaque Colonial White

Krystiania Publishing has a green profile, and
strives to publish books of natural, renewable and
recyclable materials.
The paper is acid- and lignin-free, made from
sustainable forests. Our books are CoC-certified,
by either FSC®, SFI® or PEFC™, depending on
where they are produced.

ISBN 978-82-93295-21-1

www.krystiania.com

CONTENTS

"I approach you, as you are my friend, my servant and priest
[...]. I have been rejected from the Pleroma, and it is I that
Valentinus called Sophia Achamoth. It is I that Simon Magus
called Helena-Ennoia [...].
Listen carefully: The One has produced One, and then one
more. And these three are but One: The Father, The Word and
the Thought. Establish my Gnostic Church. The Demiurge will
have no power over it. Receive the Paraclete"

Sophia-Achamoth revealing herself to Jules Doinel

PREFACE

"Spring is late this year" the bishop says, and brings me a cup of tea. I smile and glance out of the window of the nice warm apartment at the snow storm outside and the empty backyard.

Some weeks ago, I met the Gnostic bishop at a lecture in a spare at the Victorian pub Kristiania at the central station in Oslo, the Norwegian capital. I knew they used to meet at this place on social occasions, and as I have been a student of Gnostic literature for many years, he invited me to a meeting they had planned for the coming week. So this is where I am now, in a small underground church on the peaceful west side of the city.

I am sitting on the sofa, and we talk a little about Gnosticism and our personal experiences with the Gnostic myth. It is all quite informal, and during our talk more people drop in and help themselves to tea or coffee. Someone who has not had time for breakfast makes toast in the kitchen. Some bohemian looking people seem as if they came directly from yesterday's party and ask for coffee when they are still in the hall. Another person looks like a stockbroker, and one of the girls is dressed as from a gothic movie, but balances the dark velvet and makeup with a warm smile. Yet another seems as if he is going to the gym right after the meeting. It is indeed a very varied group of people.

The situation is very relaxed, and the bishop and the female priest, yes there are female priests and bishops in the Gnostic church, do not try to elevate themselves above the common participant. They are quite human and much less pontifical than other clergy I have visited.

When all have some warm beverage in their cups, the bishop leans forward to the table and says:

"From the beginning you have been immortal. You are children of the eternal life. If you had allowed death to enfold you in his realm, it would have been to annihilate and disintegrate it; to let it die in and through you. You dissolve the world but are not dissolved by it yourselves. You sovereign of all creation and destruction."

The room fell quiet, and a cunning smile ran across the bishop's lips, and several of the others look at each other nodding.

I recognize the quote, and asks if it is not one of the sayings of Valentinus? The female priest nods and explains that he was one of the great Gnoseologists (Gnostic theologians) of early Gnosticism. He is still an important source of inspiration for Gnostics of today, who continues to perpetuate his experiences in modern form. These experiences are the common ground of the Gnostic understanding, and it is conveyed through experience not through doctrinal teachings.

The conversation continues for an hour or so, on the topics of being human in the world, life and death, and the difficulties of keeping a spiritual focus in a world which is obsessed with the mundane. Listening to them, the liberty of post modernism comes to mind. It seem as if no one is afraid to forward their point of view, on pain of being put down as unintelligent or lacking in knowledge. Everyone speaks from their own experiences and their own understanding. It is not a discussion of dogma and how it should be understood. I would describe it as somewhat therapeutic and even poetic. They are so very much more pragmatic than other religious people I have encountered in my life, and if it had not been for the fact that this is a meeting in a church I would not have thought of them as believers at all (and as a matter of fact they are not believers, as they are Gnostics. Gnosis means knowledge or understanding in Greek).

At certain times during the conversation, there are some natural intervals of silence, not an uncomfortable silence but more like peace, as if everyone has had a good mouthful of rich wine and was just leaning back to enjoy the taste. I am totally fascinated by this way of interaction. It is as though patterns of understanding are emerging from the conversation rather than being structurally created argument by argument.

When the conversation is at an end, someone takes the cups to the kitchen as the bishop places a table with a white cloth against the wall. He places two large but simple candleholders with white candles on the table, and between them an old book that I later realized was the Gospel according to St. John.

In front of these there is a simple silver chalice with wine and a small plate with bread.

We, the congregation, sit wherever we see fit in the room, some on pillows, others on a sofa or just some simple chairs. The setting makes me think that this must be similar to how the Hellenistic Gnostics met in each other's apartments in Rome and Alexandria, and how the church was manifested wherever they met. A church without a regular meeting place.

And as my thoughts drifted to ancient Gnostic traditions as described by the Catholic church fathers, I became aware of a hushed discussion in a corner where the bishop and some members of the clergy decided who would officiate at the altar this time. To decide this, the bishop asked them to draw lots. The honour was granted to the bishop and a female priest. Irenaeus should have seen this, I thought with a smile on my lips.

The text of the sacrament is handed out, *Fraction du Pain*, or Breaking of Bread. This is the Eucharist of the church.

We are asked to prepare ourselves, and most of the people in the congregation closes their eyes in meditation, in order to focus on what is to come.

The clergy at the altar wears a simple robe and stole, and the woman places a thin white veil on hear head that reaches to her abdomen.

The female priest, or priestess (they do not use that phrase), kneels before the bishop and lifts the veil. The bishop draws a T between her brows and blesses her before he blesses us all.

We then sing a psalm called Beati vos Æones. Even though I do not understand the words of the psalm, as it is in Latin, it contributes greatly to the sacred atmosphere. As the psalm comes to an end, the priestess recites the Lord's Prayer in Greek. Everyone sings Amen at the end.

The Priestess continues: "Before his mystical suffering, the Jesus Eon took bread and this wine in his sacred hands, raised his eyes to the heavens, broke the bread, blessed it and gave it to his disciples as he said:"

"Eat and drink of this!"

As she speaks she breaks the bread and blesses it together with the wine.

Then she elevates the bread and says: "This is the spiritual body of Christ". She then puts the bread back on the altar and kneels for a moment in prayer. She then repeats the same procedure with the wine.

After this, the room is filled with monotonous song from some loudspeakers in the back, and she eats a piece of the bread and drinks of the wine. Then after a short time she gives bread and wine to the bishop. Then she gives it to us, the congregation. Upon receiving the sacrament we return to silent meditative prayer until we hear the priestess says: "May the blessings of the holy Pleroma forever be upon you".

And the bishop blesses us with a final gnostic blessing.

It is all done in no more than half an hour, but the experience leaves an atmosphere of beauty and peace. Even so, it had also awoken a hunger for more knowledge in me and I was pleased to be able to satisfy this need before I had to leave the city.

The morning had become evening and some of the guests had

obligations waiting for them out in the snow storm. This left us with a company of five, who settled for an early weekend dinner with memorable Italian wine.

The Gnosticism I had been acquainted with, was the Gnosticism described by the Catholic church fathers in their antagonistic writings, and the books from the Nag Hammadi Library. I did also know about Gnostics performing Catholic inspired masses, but had no idea that there existed something like this. And when I ask the bishop how this particular brand of Gnosticism came to be, his face had a vacant expression before he says that a fulfilling answer to that question would be both complicated and time consuming, but he told me it all begun with a French librarian whose name was Jules Doinel in the second half of the eighteen hundreds. And that the tale of his life and how the Eglise Gnostique was established would take a whole evening or would be enough to fill a book for that matter.

- Anonymous guest

****

***

*

...or a book for that matter...

As I was at the dinner that early spring evening, I took it upon myself to tell the tale of Jules Doinel and the Eglise Gnostique – about the man, the church, the sacrament and the teachings.

A friend of mine asked the anonymous guest if she would be so kind to write down her experiences from the day she was at the church. I thought it would serve as a good eye witness description of a typical meeting in this Gnostic fellowship. And as you see from what you have just read she concurred.

To Ennoia...

FOREWORD

" Since the middle of the nineties,
when I first encountered the Gnostic writings,
I have made this world view my own.
And I have tried to remain in the awareness
of the fullness in the eternal moment,
as a key to self, life, inspiration
and the good things in life."

- A modern Gnostic

In this book, I seek to describe the first modern Gnostic church, a church established long after the abolition of Gnosticism and the persecution of its teachers and followers in the early part of the European dark ages. The age of catholic hegemony in all questions regarding faith, philosophy and world view was then imposed.

It is important for me to clarify that my intention is to describe this first Gnostic Church in an unbiased way, even though I sympathize with the Gnostic world view. I think, however, the original material in this book speaks for itself regarding the mission of this organization.

The first part of the book gives a biographical sketch of Jules Doinel who was the founder of the restored Gnostic church tradition at the end of the 19th century. By describing his life, I also describe the events leading to the birth of the Eglise Gnostique as these are closely related to each other. Doinel was a visionary and may even be regarded as a Gnostic prophet, as his visions and experiences paved the way for the restoration of the Gnostic tradition as a church structure. He, like other prophets, has received revelations that have led to the foundation of religions or reforms.

In the second part of the book there is a catechism that was supposed to be used in the early years of the new church, but was never completed. It was therefore published some years later in the journal *La Gnose* in 1910. This catechism gives a good impression of the teachings and the structure of the Gnosticism of Doinel.

In the third part the sacraments of the church are presented in their full form. They have previously been published, according to Doinel's wishes, but have been out of print for the last ten years or so. The material for this translation is taken from the French originals stored in the archive of the Martinist order *Ordre Reaux Croix* in Oslo. I am grateful for their help with this project.

The sacraments reveal how the teachings that are described in the catechism are used by the Gnostics as self-redemptive mechanisms. The church and the mythology thus constitute the working space and the tools of the trade. Rituals and structures are pragmatic means to a higher end.

In the last part of the book are some doctrinal core texts by Doinel. These are homilies, lectures and instructions. These texts may broaden the understanding of the reader regarding the teachings of the church. These texts are chosen as they are considered classical texts of Doinel. He also wrote on other topics such as French heroes and the ancient Egypt.

For those who have no previous acquaintance with Gnosticism or Gnostic church activity, I would recommend them to begin with *The Valentinian Gnosticism* in this part of the book and then continue with the *Gnostic catechism*. This will give the necessary foundation for being able to enjoy the rest of the book.

Collecting data on historic facts

To me working on this book has been a personal journey into deeper understanding of the neo-Gnostic movement and its different institutions from its foundation up to our present time. Even though I see the benefit of church institutions as vehicles for Gnostic teachings, I do also see that there is a downside to this approach. Gnosis is a special kind of self-knowledge that aids people in their personal growth, it is meant to liberate the mind from unhealthy attachments, useless customs and obsessive behaviours that make it difficult to experience the fullness of the present and the mystery of reality. There is always a polarity between tradition and flexibility, and this may be even clearer as time goes by. And all this comes down to the people carrying on the tradition today. Church hierarchies and historic legacies, epic titles and divine teachings are conveyed through initiations and the art of storytelling; and all of this is perpetuated by humans. Ordinary humans in extraordinary situations.

It may be important to concider that several Gnostics view both the church and the sacraments as tools in a personal Gnostic process, not independent goals. This is the challenge that has haunted the Gnostic churches (and other religious societies as well) through history. Individuals seeking redemption from the clutches of the ego may in the end become custodians of the traditional structure and protectors of their own titles and power. This may twist the Gnostic quest into being all about historical structures, promoting titles and fighting over patriarch titles and legitimacy.

In writing this book, the most difficult part was to describe the history. The source material has consisted of manuscripts, books and dialogues with Gnostic clergy. Both material and living sources included personal likes, dislikes and opinions connected to the Doinel tradition and what actually happened. This may be a source of bias.

I have tried to describe the history without evaluating who was right or who was wrong. I leave this to those who need to make such distinctions.

Rune Ødegaard
Oslo, Autumn Equinox , 2017
128 years after the Gnostic restoration ...

Regarding the translations

During the translation process I made some decisions which I hope will clarify the material. When I talk about the female equivalent of bishop the name Sophia is usually used. However, occasionally this office has also been described using the name Sophial. In order not to confuse this office with the spiritual entity Sophia I have chosen to use the name Sophial.

Perfect (*Parfait*), the church's priesthood, is translated to *perfecti*. I have not made any distinction between the male and the female form of this terminology, even though this occasionally occurs in the French texts.

The Paraclet is a term used in this material referring to the Holy Spirit. Paraclet means helper or spokesman. In the Gospel according to St. John, the author writes that the Paraclet will come in the absence of Jesus, in order to support and guide the disciples (Joh. 14,16.26; 15,26; 16,7).

In the sacraments, I have moved the instructions for the participants' clothing and the outlay of the room to the beginning of each text. I have also included the prayer as a whole where the instructions have said only recite e. g. the Paternoster. This is done so the reader can more easily imagine the course of the sacraments.

I would like to apologize in advance for what might be lost in translation as my first language is not French, even though I have had thorough help from several individuals who are French speaking. I would also like to invite people, in the light of the tradition, to contribute more and better translations in the future. I also welcome any inputs people may have concerning texts they believe should have been included in this translation, that I have had to omit due to my choice of selection. Those texts might be included in potentially later editions of this book.

I have roughly kept the same paragraphs and layout as the texts had in the original French editions. I have however taken into account the aesthetic when the formatting of the text is characterized by being originally published in a journal.

I sincerely hope that, through this, you as a reader will enjoy reading this book and through its material will contribute to a deeper understanding of the neo-Gnostic church as an organization as well as its own theology.

Thanks to:
every one of you who
contributed towards this book's existence,
my beloved wife Kjersti, my friends
Marianne, Matts, Howard, Sølvi, Joachim and James,
and all my fellow accomplices in Krystiania Publishing,
and to every gnostic who shares their knowledge
and who walk the path with fellow wanderers
who dedicate their lives to knowledge
rather than acknowledgment...

HISTORY

Jules Doinel

Childhood and adolescence

Jules Doinel was born on the 8th December 1842 in Moulins, Allier, France. His full name was Jules-Benoît Stanislas Doinel du Val-Michel, but in most of the written work he left behind, he refers to himself as Jules Doinel. He has occasionally signed his work using Jean Kostka, Novalis, Kostka Borgia, Jules Stanislas Doinel, Stany Doinel Jules and Jules Doinel du Val-Michel. His parents, Luis and Marie Honoré Doinel, were deeply religious Catholics which gave Jules a strong connection with the practices and belief of the church early in his life.

Throughout his childhood he experienced visionary episodes like lying awake dreaming, where he saw historical events or visions for which he had no rational explanation. Sometimes it involved dreams of epic tales from Hesiod to a defining moment involving a massive vulture which appeared above his bed one evening. All the dream visions had a sort of ghostly feel to them. The awake dreams occasionally consisted of sounds and voices and usually they were initiated by an unaccountable sound of music. This music, he later thought, was connected to the *harmonious music of the spheres*, some sort of celestial music experience.

In 1853, when he was 11 years old, he started attending a Jesuit school not far from his childhood home. At age 17 he became novice in the order. The visions followed him through his time as an apprentice. One time, whilst praying in the chapel, a snow white beam of light descended from above and illuminated the monstrance on the alter, thus giving him a clear feeling of a divine presence. At this point the visions were closely connected to religious events and images and he would meet saints and clergy who would converse with him. He would also meet deceased people who would ask him for favours or tell him details about unfinished business from their lives.

He abandoned his career within the Jesuit school only a year after he started it, so he could leave his home town. Doinel moved from the familiar area where he grew up to the capital, Paris, where he completed his college education at Collège Stanislas. This lead to him being accepted at l'École des Chartes in 1862 and he was awarded his diploma in 1866 after writing a thesis on Jerusalem's patriarchs with the title *"Essai sur la vie et les principales œuvres de Pierre de la Palu, patriarche de Jérusalem, 1275 ou 1280-1342."* He was at that time 24 years old and already an experienced writer with a keen interest in the spiritual. He then obtained his first job as an archivist and started his involvement with the contemporary practice of spiritualism. His interest in spiritualism, most likely, is an result of all his visions. The practice of spiritualism was well regarded and highly popular in all corners of society during this time period. Doinel would have been regarded as a highly developed medium for the spiritual.

In 1869, he got married to Stephanie-Françoise Le Clerc, with whom he had a deep affectionate relationship, but sadly she passed away in 1873.

In the period leading up to 1870 he had several positions as an archivist whilst writing texts as well as books on the subject of medieval history. Some of the themes included in his writings were of Joan of Arc, Blanche of Castile, Hugues Le Bouteiller and the crusades. His entire professional life was involved with being an archivist at several places, thus giving him access to a huge amount of historical material which was not known nor available to others.

But it would not be these early texts on history nor his work as an archivist that would make Jules Doinel's mark on history. What made Jules Doinel known were the circumstances that took place while he was working at the archives at Loiret and the experiences that led up to the divine meeting with an apostolic age old Christian tradition.

FREEMASONS, SALONS AND GNOSTICISM

In 1874 Jules married Marie-Louise Clemence Chaigneau who introduced him to the Masonic community and the social life. Ten years later he was accepted and initiated into the Masonic lodge, *Emules de Montyon*. Masonic lodges were seen as the complete opposite of the Catholic Church which prohibited any Masonic involvement. Doinel served as a speaker in his mother-lodge from 1886 to 1893.

During this period of transition, Jules studied the teachings of a reform pastor who went by the name Guillaume Monod. This religious relationship may have been what started the transition from Catholicism to his engagement in a much older Christian tradition.

The three basic Masonic degrees, Entered Apprentice, Fellowcraft and Master Mason, did not make any significant impression on Doinel. On the other hand the high degrees of Freemasonry did, particularly the degree called *Chevalier de Rose-Croix*, the Knight of the Rosy Cross.

The high degrees inspired him to study the Isis mysteries and he experienced several visions of this Egyptian goddess as well as interactions with her.

In 1885 Marie-Louise Clemence Chaigneau gave birth to his son who was baptized by the reformed pastor Monod.

Circumstances were about to change for Doinel, and the biggest indication of this happened in 1888. This was the year Doinel supposedly found the manuscript dating back to 1022. This manuscript was, according to Doinel, written by a Gnostic teacher by the name of Canon Stephan de Orléans who was burnt for heresy that same year. However, no one has been able to confirm the existence of such a document. While working at the Loiret he found several documents linked to the Church of the Cathars, who once flourished in Southern France, where they still operate. The history and ideas of the Cathar Church were very popular among esoteric circles in Paris during this time. Doinel was not alone in his fascination with the Cathar history and heritage. However, it was an important backdrop to the prevalence of the movement Doinel was about to put in motion.

In the Cathar version of Christianity they taught that the evil material world was created by the *Old Testament's* false creator God and considered Satan the ruler of this world. The human purpose and aim was therefore to let go of the chains of the material world. When Jesus came into the world it was, according to their writings, to preach the teachings of the true God, the God beyond all of creation. The Cathar religious community was well organised with priests called perfecti and their own bishops. The services took place in the homes of the congregation, thus leaving them independent of any need for church premises.

They also had their own sacrament that was supposed to contribute to the redemption from the world and the power of the ruler of the world - this was called the *Consolamentum*. The Consolamentum made the receivers free from all sin and devoted them to becoming perfecti themselves. The Cathars lived a simple and thrifty life which was the complete opposite of the Catholic Church's enormous wealth and worldly power.

The Pope called a formal crusade against the Cathars, the Albigensian crusade, in 1208. This was named after the town of Albi which was inhabited by a large number of Cathars. This led to a tremendous massacre of men and women of all ages in the attempt to annihilate what they called the Albigensian heresy. The last known perfectis of that era were executed in Languedoc in 1321.

Through the systematical extermination of the Cathars the Pope intended all their texts to be destroyed. Besides the *New Testament*, they also used the scriptures *The Gospel of the Secret Supper, Interrogation of John* and *The Book of Two Principles*. There is little information concerning the survival of complete copies of the scriptures and, if not held by private collectors, we may assume they are lost.

It might have been fragments of these texts or of the Consolamentum that was the sacrament that Jules Doinel found while working in the archive. He was also concerned with other early Christian movements with similarities to Catharism like the Manicheans and the Bogomils. These movement have all been described as Gnostic. Doinel was passionately devoted to this early Christian theology and all its shaped and forms.

To give a short definition of Gnosticism is not easy as Gnosticism is a collective term for a number or traditions, but they did however have, as Doinel also points out in Catharism in this book, some commonalities. These commonalities is the teachings of emanation in contrary to creation and redemption or salvation through acknowledgement in opposition to faith or belief.

Emanation is a central consept, and the Great Norwegian Encyclopaedia explains the word as follows:

> "You can imagine the world occurred by an emanation
> from God, who is not seen as a personified being, but
> a divine substance which constantly exceeds its limits.
> The doctrine is in direct opposition to both the Judeo-
> Christian creation story, where the world is created by

the act of God, and to the evolution theory where the world has evolved from a lower form of existence into a higher form. In emanation, the ratio is reversed - the perfect divine substance is flooding over and becoming the imperfect world."

Gnosticism is however most known for the doctrine of the world being created by a semi-creator, a Demiurge who is not as predominantly evil as the Cathars' world creator. The concept of a Demiurge was introduced in Plato's "Timaios", and ever since its creator has been given different traits. These can vary from the creator as an aggressive and vindictive prison guard to representations resembling a good-hearted but siple minded artisan.

It is important to understand that the Christian Gnostics probably did not have the same relationship towards their scriptures as the predecessors of the Catholic church, or today's dogma oriented Christianity. The reason for this is that the Gnostics constantly wrote new scriptures and rituals for their congregations. It appears as if they used the myths in more of a therapeutic manner than as a theological and scientific reality. If that is the case they were much more forward-looking than the political oriented Christians who were inspired to champion one church and one faith and then criminalize all others.

Doinel's studies of Gnosticism included all the sources to which he had access. Mainly the Church Fathers' descriptions of their opponents. However, their descriptions were very extensive. Ironically, they were so extensive that they gave a thorough overview of the Gnostic doctrine and soul. Doinel was particularly interested in Simon Magus and Valentinus. Valentinus (c. AD 100 to about AD160) was one of the first of early Christianity's systematical theologians. It was Valentinus who established what would to be called The Valentinian

Gnosticism or Valentinianism. Simon Magus is said to be the legendary founder of Gnosticism and his companion, Helena, was a manifestation of God's consciousness, Ennoia. Ennoia is a form of divine infinitive entity, a more transcendent size than Isis, who also fascinated Doinel.

Doinel wanted to unite the teachings of Simon Magus and Valentinus , but he found this to be quite challenging regarding the ritual and sacramental practices. This was because there only existed very unlikely and somewhat incomplete descriptions of the rituals.

Whilst he immersed himself in Gnosticism he had several Gnostic visions. One of these appeared during a meeting in the Rose-Croix degree of the Ancient & Accepted Rite of Freemasonry. He saw the letters INRI written on the cross in front of him and they were filled by an inner spirit which gave them life. They were transformed into a three-dimensional form and grew larger in the room, chanting: "INRI, *Ignis Natura Renovatur Integra,* through fire, nature is reborn. God is the fire. Through conveying the teachings of Simon Magus shall you possess Helena".

More visions followed of Ennoia, where she appeared as a beautiful blond woman. He had a second vision during a Masonic meeting where he saw the roof being covered by more and more stars until they spelled out the Greek name for Ennoia, followed by the sound of the words " *In Cathedra Gnostica Mulier Prophetica Revelatur homini[1]*" dominating his entire inner hearing.

After having studied Egyptology, Freemasonry and the Gnostic material to which he had access, he concluded that the true Masonic beliefs and origins constituted Gnosticism.

It is interesting that some important Masonic authorities also shared this view, independent from any visions or revelations.

---

1 The woman on the throne reveals the Gnostic prophecies to man.

Albert Pike, leader of the southern jurisdiction of the *Ancient and Accepted Scottish Rite of Freemasonry* in the US, also had a similar view, and in Norway Niels Trescow, a prominent mason of the *Swedish rite*, expressed this in his writings.

The great vision and revelation appeared to Jules Doinel later that year. In this vision he met Jesus who told him that he would be the founder of a new church.

He was then 46 years old.

THE RETURN OF GNOSIS

On one late evening in 1888, Doinel had a very special vision, it was a calling that would fundamentally change his life. In this vision he saw Jesus as an aeon, a being of eternity. He was ordained by Jesus Christ and two Bogomil bishops who assisted with the ceremony. He was made *Bishop of Montségur* and an *Albigensian patriarch*. After the ordination ceremony, Jesus Christ instructed him to establish a new church.

The year 1888 was of importance in European esoteric history in several ways. At the same time as Doinel had his vision in France, the three Freemasons and Rosicrucians William Robert Woodman, William Wynn Westcott and Samuel Liddell MacGregor Mathers established the *Hermetic Order of the Golden Dawn* in England. This would later be described as one of the most, important and most influential occult orders in Northern Europe. The order has today many branches and the doctrine is still a benchmark. In France Marquis Stanislas de Guaita established *L'Ordre Kabbalistique de la Rose Croix* as an esoteric university and junction for members of different French and European orders.

Marie de Mariategiu, Lady Caithness,
Duchess of Medina Pomars.

Spiritualism and the visions were still the main spiritual tool used by Doinel and he attended séances held in the salon of Marie de Mariategiu, Lady Caithness, Duchess of Medina Pomars. The Duchess and her circle had connections with the *Theosophical Society*, and had been instructed by the leader of this organisation, Helena Petrovna Blavatsky, to establish theosophy in France. She had a strong confidence in spiritism and the messages conveyed through it. Messages through these séances had told her that she was a reincarnation of Mary Stuart of the Scottish royal family. The Duchess and Doinel became deeply connected and were each other's counterpart.

He admired her knowledge, esoteric abilities and social position. She admired him as an outstanding medium. It is also a possibility that Doinel concidered her a manifestation of Ennoia. This was, however, an honour she would not accept. There can be several reasons why, but one of them could be that she through metaphysical logic had to be a reincarnation of the prostitute Helena that Simon delivered from a brothel, a thought that would probably have been less desirable than being a reincarnation of Mary Stuart.

Doinel's seances with the Duchess aroused an interest in France and international esoteric communities. Several important members of different orders participated. After his vision and ordination Doinel consequently used the seances in which he participated to seek deeper insight into the Gnostic knowledge he had been handed. It appears that Doinel used spiritism to further develop his understanding of the mandate he had received.

Doinel often had contact with *Sophia-Achamoth*. Sophia is Greek for wisdom and Sophia-Achamoth was, according to the gnostic theologian Valentinus, the fallen wisdom or the higher wisdom's daughter and the unfortunate mother of the demiurge, or the capricious world creator. Sophia-Achamoth is the lower aspect of Ennoia. The message one evening was:

> "I am addressing you because you are my friend, my servant and priest in my Albigensian Church. I have been rejected from the Pleroma, and it is I whom Valentinus named Sophia-Achamoth. It is I whom Simon Magus called Helena-Ennoia, I am the eternal androgyne. Jesus is the word of God, I am the thought of God. One day I shall return to my Father in the highest, but to achieve this I need assistance. I need my brother Jesus's intervention, to intercede for me. Only the Infinite can redeem the Infinite, only God can redeem God.
> Listen carefully: "The One has brought forth One, then One more. And the three are but One, The Father, The Word and The Thought. Establish my Gnostic Church. The Demiurge will be powerless over it. Receive the Paraclete."

Doinel was convinced that his life mission was to restore the divine feminine and to establish the fallen Sophia's church on earth. The following year, the spiritist circle contacted a spiritual synod of 40 Cathar bishops, Bishops of the Paraclete.

BISHOPS OF THE PARACLETE

The following text is Doinel's own descriptions of what took place one autumn evening towards the end of the nineteenth century: -

During this gathering at Lady C. autumn 188x so incredible and significant revelation took place that you can date the restoration of the Gnostic church to this day and this month. I will be faithful in my approach and respect the custom by not naming the people present.

The oratory was dimly lit by the scented lamp the noblewoman constantly let burn in front of the painting of Mary Stuart. Alone in the mysterious gloom the royal portrait clearly stood out, highlighting her golden pale skin.

The oratory was a secluded room in the middle of Paris's own Hollywood, a room completely dedicated to Lady C's precious memories, well organised for supernatural influences. The noise from the street never entered the room and a heavy curtain separated the room from the enormous library in front of it. The walls were simple and the furniture was rare and covered with occult symbols. Its own ornate alcove was arranged behind the Shrine to accommodate the inspiring painting. The oratory was a cabinet of evocation, nothing less than an intimate chapel. An aura floated above the arcadian canopies. I have always felt I have had to whisper when I am in the temple. People with experiences from occult meetings will easily recognize this subtle feeling that you must experience to understand.

The participants were as if drowned in a sedative liquid, their brains were saturated with sedative movements and their eyes melted into a hallucinogenic steam. It was as if bound together by the joints and the heart was compressed, a compression that does not hurt but paralyses.

In the middle of the oratory, which has become legendary, a heavy, massive and spherical wooden table with a three-legged chair was installed to be used during evocations. This was the furniture in the middle of the room and one could understand that this was the base for the oracle's travels.

We formed a ring around this sybilline table, which was without cover from any fabric and which massive distorted spiral legs resembling the ominous legs of some sphinxes who were awakened from their dreams.

The distinguished company, who had been summoned for this illustrious and solemn gathering, knew the means and the reason for their gathering. One of the gentlemen present had passed away, but there were also a Spanish grandee present, also six foreign mystics, aristocratic aroused and highly intelligent women, six occult inquisitive Eves.

It is important to point out that a powerful medium was to be the instrument for the forces and a channel for the revelations. I should immediately explain about my own spiritual state, as this is essential to understand what was about to happen. I was looking for the religious formula for contact with the absolute, my heart desired boundless emotions, the imagination was hunting for idealistic visions, the spirit thirsty for the teachings of the light, and I wanted to realize them and incorporate them in a representation of a higher metaphysical state and manifest them in a cult strong enough to replace the Catholic church. In one word, I wanted to resurrect Gnosticism. On this memorable occasion, the noble evocator wanted to aid me and the assembly that was to be, by consulting with the spirits of the old Albigensian bishops who were overcome by the crusaders led by Simon de Montfort.

Consequently, we were waiting for a manifestation from the ancient Paraclete church. It was almost ten o'clock. After a period of silence and a long silent prayer, the heavy table started to quiver beneath our fingers. It was almost as if life once again started to circulate through the veins of the wood and made it alive. A quaint modulation ran in loud waves of a massive depth. It was immensely powerful and it made everyone very excited. It sounded like the melody 'Is Deus in nobis, agitante calescimus illo'[2]. The lifeless material lent its form mysteriously to the forces in action.

The medium made a gesture to Lady C. She then grabbed the staff of evocation and brought it over an alphabetical dial. And as the staff passed more rapidly over the letters in relief, brief and clear knocks could be heard. She spelled out the following sentence:

> Prepare, soon the bishops of the Albigensian synod of Montségur will arrive.

Simultaneously a sudden flash of light sparkled from all corners of the walls in the oratory. The portrait of Mary came to life, a smile roamed her painted lips and phosphorus essence sparkled in her eyes. I could not contain my scream. Mary Queen of Scots appeared to be alive.

Another silence more intense than the last one, more profound and expressive, spread around the enchanted oratory. A cold breath caressed my forehead and I felt a firm but soft hand on my knee. The hairs on my head stood up while the wind from the invisible brushed my hair. I looked over to the woman next to me, Countess X, and my neighbour to the left, Princess X. They were pale, extremely pale. The strained nerves trembled and we were undoubtedly under the influence of something.

Then a slow and mute rhythm arouse from the table. It turned

---

2 Quote from Ovid: There is a God in us that makes us incited.

into a conscious being. The table slammed against the floor and the rhythm increased in both sound and resonance while it marked and accentuated the rhythm. It made it richer as if it were two drummers playing the theme.

This went on for at least ten long minutes and when the triumphant rhythmical march ended, a powerful beat rang out from the middle of the table, and the staff again brushed over the alphabetical dial.

These words were spelled out in a magical manner:

> Guilhabert de Castres, Bishop of Montségur, and the 40 Bishops of the cardinal synod are here.

An irresistible impulse made us all stand up and the evocation commenced. First of with the prayer to the Paraclete, then greetings to the Gnostic bishops and finally the portentous questioning.

I do not recall the exact words, but I can guarantee the meaning in the rendition of the magical communication. It was Guilhabert de Castres who talked and he told us the following:

> We have come forth to you from the circle that has been removed from the two Empyrians and we bless you.
> May the principle of good, God, forever be promised blessed, praised and worshipped. Amen.
> We have come forth to you, our beloved. You, Valentin, you shall institute the assembly of the Paraclete and will call it the Église Gnostique. I proclaim to you that you shall take Helena as assistant in spirit and you shall be engaged to her. You shall be her husband and she shall be your spouse. Together you shall appoint your bishops and you will ordain them in accordance with the Gnostic rite. You, Valentin, you shall be holy in the

oratory. You shall reinstate and teach the Gnostic doctrine, the absolute doctrine. You shall use the fourth gospel, that of St. John as the gospel, for it is the gospel of love. The congregation shall consist of male and female perfecti. The Holy Spirit will send you the ones who must be sent to you. We bring joy and peace, the joy of the spirits and the peace of the heart.

Kneel now, you who are the first fruits of Gnosis and we will bless you.

An easily understood feeling filled us, tears flooded to our eyes, and an apprehension, delightful yet mild, took hold in our hearts. I felt a burning fire circulating through my veins. We knelt down while, yet again, the table started its rhythmical song, an aura surrounded us like a whirlpool and a powerful voice proclaimed:

May the Holy Pleroma bless you, may the Aeons bless you. We bless you as we blessed the martyrs of the Pyrenean Thabor.

Amen. Amen. Amen.

All sound stopped abruptly and the table went silent. The magical portrait was once again a lifeless figure.

We got up, exhausted and trembling. The revelation was over.

The Bishops of the Paraclete had vanished.

This was the beginning of the Era of the Gnosis Restored.[3]

The leader for this synod was, according to the revelations, Guilhabert de Castres. He was a prominent teacher and Cathar bishop of Toulouse, whom live from c. 1165 to c. 1240.

---

3 Description is taken from *Lucifer Démasque* (1895), written by Jules Doinel

The seal of Jules Doinel

Doinel declared the Era of the Gnosis Restored and the Église Gnostique was established 21st September 1890.

A DENOMINATION TAKES FORM

As the Jesus-aeon and the bishops had dictated, Doinel assumed the office as Patriarch for the Gnostic Church. This church used the name the Church of the Paraclete but mostly it was known as Église Gnostique, and it is this name by which the church is known to this day.

As a bishop, he used the name Valentin II, to show his affiliation to, and as a extension of, Valentinian tradition and Gnosticism.

Later he became a member of the Martinist Order, which is based on the teachings of Louis-Claude de Saint-Martin (1743-1803), a mystic from Amboise. This doctrine may be summarized in a quote, translated and published on the homepage of the Martinist order *Ordre Reaux Croix* (www.ordrereauxcroix.org).

> "The only initiation which I advocate and which I look for with all the ardour of my Soul, is that by which we are able to enter into the Heart of God within us, and there make an Indissoluble Marriage, which makes us the Friend, the Brother and Spouse of the Repairer … there is no other way to arrive at this Holy Initiation than for us to delve more and more into the depth of our Soul and not let go of the prize until we have succeeded in liberating its lively and vivifying origin."
>
> -Louis-Claude de Saint-Martin

It is however interesting that the French esoteric authority Robert Amadou thought there were reasons to claim that the origin of the teachings of Saint-Martin and his initiator

Joachim Don Martinez de Pasqually (1710-1774), derived from Valentinianism. Valentinianism is partly apparent and partly hidden in the text *Traité sur la réintégration des êtres dans leur première propriété, vertu et puissance spirituelle divine.*

It was natural to ordain more bishops and Sophials (Sophia or Sophials as mentioned earlier was the title used for female bishops.)

The three bishops that were ordained in the first stages amounted to the first synod, or the Very High Synod.

It consisted of Gérard Encausse, Paul Sédir and Lucien Chamuel.

Gérard Encausse

Gérard Encausse, also known as Papus, took the mystical name Tau Vincent (14th of September 1892), and became bishop of Toulouse. Encausse was born in Corunna, Spain, in 1865. Early on in life he studied Kabbala, tarot and alchemy. He obtained a degree to become a Doctor. He affiliated with several orders, some of them were *L'Ordre Kabbalistique de la Rose Croix, The Hermetic Order of the Golden Dawn, Hermetic Brotherhood of Luxor* and the *Antient and Primitive Rite of Memphis and Mizraim*. He was also the first Grand Master of the Martinist Order and it was through its journal, *L'Initiation,* that Doinel published many of the church texts.

As well as being a doctor Encausse was a known author within esoteric circles and wrote many books thoughout his life. From an historical curiosity point of view it is worth mentioning his personal friendship with Tsar Nicholas II of Russia and Tsarina Alexandra.

Paul Sédir

Paul Sédir, also known as Yvon Le Loup, took the mystical name Tau Paul and was coadjutor, or second bishop of Toulouse.

Sédir was born in Bretagne in 1871, but grew up in Paris.

He was a banker by profession, working in The Bank of France through most of his career. But behind this bank worker there was a dedicated student of the esoteric. In 1889, 18 years old, he met the 25 year old Encausse at a meeting in the bookstore *La Librairie du Merveilleux*, and they became close friends and continued their esoteric work together. Sédir became a member of the same orders as Encausse and was part of the governing body in several of these. Later in life Christian mysticism became the most important element in his personal esoteric work.

Lucien Chamuel

Lucien Chamuel, also known as Lucien Mauchel, assumed the mystical name Tau Bardesanes, and became the bishop of La Rochelle and Saintes.

Chaumel came from the Vendée in France and studied law. He was also an esoteric student and a friend of Encausse. At one point Encausse is supposed to have asked him if 100 francs was enough to establish a publishing house and a book store. The result of this conversation was La Librairie du Merveilleux. La Librairie du Merveilleux became a great success and attracted many esotericists, Freemasons, artists, poets and café philosophers. This is where he became a good friend of Sédir. Chamuel was also a member of the same orders as Encausse and Sédir as well as an authority figure in several of these.

It is an interesting fact that these three were installed as pioneers of the Gnostic Church as they were involved in the management of several orders in France at that time, amongst them being *L'Ordre Kabbalistique de la Rose Croix, L'Ordre Martiniste* and *the Hermetic Brotherhood of Luxor*. As a result of this, as Doinel might have intended, the Gnostic church became the typical church affiliation for many of the members of the newly ordained bishops' organizations. With *L'Ordre Martiniste,* a formal corporation later developed where Église Gnostique became the Order's stated church.

Marie Chauvel became the first Sophial and assumed the name Esclarmonde after one of the great Cathar heroines. She became Sophial of Warsaw, Poland.

CONVERSIONS

Even the first years of the new church was said to have been relatively turbulent. The main reason for this turbulence was Doinel's unstable and somewhat petulant mood.

In the beginning of 1895 Doinel encountered a personal crisis. He started to question if his visions were of a true nature or if they could be the work of the Devil. He was afraid he had turned away from Catholic salvation. As before, his visions supported his thoughts and this time they were filled with harsh angels and alternations in the Ennoia-figure which he interpreted as devilish. It seems as if he was haunted by his childhood beliefs.

This crisis and the following collapse made him resign from the Gnostic church and all other orders of which he was a part. He then converted back to Catholicism.

During this period he criticized his own church and claimed that Ennoia or Sophia-Achmeta in reality were Lucifer and reinterpreted all previous understanding of Gnosic love and Gnosis to mean desires and confusion.

It is highly likely the Palladium incident, an incident closely connected to a person by the name of G.A. Jogand-Pages, had triggered Doinel's crisis.

G.A. Jogand-Pages, better known as Leo Taxil, was a former Freemason who had become an important and infamous anti-Masonry propagandist. He described what he meant by the true nature and origin of the orders and societies .

According to Taxil, all the Masonic orders were controlled by a satanic organization called the *Palladium order*[4]. And the leader of this order was Albert Pike, who was the leader of the Southern Jurisdiction of the *Ancient and Accepted Scottish Rite* of Freemasonry in the US.

---

4 The name stems from the Pallas Athena, the Greek Goddess of Wisdom.

Like most conspiracy theorists within this field, he claimed the order controlled everything and everybody and that their ceremonies consisted of orgies, devil worshipping and scarifications of infants. It was this scenario of horrors that might have led Doinel to turn away from everything he had built and to write the book *Lucifer Démasqué* the same year, under the pseudonym Jean Kosta.

In 1897 Taxil confessed to making up the whole case of the Palladium order and his so called informant whom had given him all his 'facts' had been his own secretary.

This turned out to be an embarrassing affair for his believers and especially the Catholic church which had embraced him.

This situation left Doinel in a vacuum that led him back to the Gnosticism he had abandoned.

Lucifer Démasqué (1895), written by Doinel under the pseudonym Jean Kostka

A NEW PATRIARCH

While all this was happening, the Gnostic Church did not have any tremendous reaction to Doinel's abandonment and conversion back to Catholicism. Gérard Encausse, from the synod, commented on this by saying that Doinel was wobbling between conversion and insanity, and that he was grateful that the former patriarch had chosen conversion.

The same year as Doinel left the church, the synod once again assembled in Maria de Mariaeguis's salon. The salon still was a central meeting point for the Gnostics. It had been the place of revelation where most of the information regarding the restoration of the church took place only a few years earlier. At this meeting, the Gnostic bishop Léonce-Eugène Joseph Fabre des Essart (1848-1917) was elected as their new patriarch. His mystical name was Synésius.

Fabre des Essarts was a poet in the French symbolism movement. He was also a long-time member esoteric societies and orders, which had made him a natural leader within these circles.

After being chosen as the patriarch, he was the driving force to develop the church doctrine further by introducing new elements. The reason for this might have been the fact that they had already used all the Gnostic material to which they had access. Instead of further developing the teachings of Simon Magus and Valentinus, as Doinel did, he gradually introduced elements which were seen as close disciplines, amongst them Taoist and Sufi elements. During this period a diplomatic effort was made to align with other churches with similar philosophy and principles.

This mixture of doctrine, affiliations and the publication of the gnostic writing *Pistis Sophia*, in 1895, led to a need for clarification.

The answer was a comprehensive catechism written by Dr. Louis-Sophrone Fugairon, under the mystical name Sophronius. Fugairon was an important writer and developer of the church and he can almost be seen as a doctor ecclesia in the former neo-Gnostic Church.

The catechism was called *Catéchisme Expliqué de L'Église Gnostique*, and consisted of 400 pages, published in 1899. Again the focus was back on Simon Magus and Valentinianism.

Léonce-Eugène Joseph Fabre des Essarts (1848-1917)

DOINEL RETURNS

In 1899 Doinel got back in touch with the church and Fabre des Essarts and in 1900 he was back in the Gnostic congregation. He was ordained as bishop of Alet and Mirepoix and he took the name Jules.

Jules Doinel died during the night of the 16th of March 1903. People who were with him state that it was unclear whether he died as a Gnostic or as a Catholic.

Doinel enters esoteric history as the founder of modern Gnosticism. Whether he was driven by inspiration, his own creative hand, higher forces or dead Cathars is insignificant from a Gnostic point of view. What is important is the gate Doinel opened to the new Gnostic era, through which many have since travelled, and are still travelling, regardless of whether Doinel was ever one of them.

Statue of Ennoia in Ephesus

DECREE & CATECHISM

A GNOSTIC CATECHISM

The Gnostics of the Église Gnostique belonged to several esoteric orders and societies with a multitude of teachings, practices and cultures. In the beginning, the backbone of the church seems to have been the sacraments and the lectures written by Jules Doinel. The creed was simple and consisted of a single sentence: "I confess to the doctrine of Emanation and redemption through Gnosis.".

The situation of the organization may have called for a more elaborate description of the particularity of the church. A catechism could be a way of presenting what they meant by the rather broad concept of Gnosticism. Further it could describe the structure of the church and its doctrine. The Decree in this chapter was written only years before Doinel's spiritual crisis. In this text he describes the fundament of the church, the Gospel according to St. John as the main gospel, the sacraments and the close relationship to the Martinist Order. This relationship also gave the Grand Master of this order, Gerard Encausse, and his closest circle, massive influence within the church. Due to this the Eglise Gnostique did not base its existence solely on Doinel any longer. It had outgrown any one person.

Doinel never finished the cathechism. Paul Sédir continued to work on it where Doinel had left off. It is included here in this book in the state it was originally published by La Gnose about one hundred years ago.

I have included it in this book, even though it was never finished, as it gives a good expression of what the leaders of this church considered to be the core teachings of Gnosticism in its early years. We do not know if it ever became a regular part of the religious life of the Gnostics in Église Gnostique.

A catechism may be viewed as unfit for the spirit of Gnosticism, due to its non-dogmatic nature. It may however be considered as a minimum standard, to generate some landmarks to gather the congregation and form a Gnostic religious culture and identity.

RESTORATION OF THE GNOSIS

Decree of the synod

The Holy Synod enacts:

FIRST ARTICLE
The re-establishment of the hierarchy permits the restoration of Gnostic symbolism.

ART. II
The Consolamentum, the Breaking of Bread and the Appareillamentum of the Albigensian assembly are restored.

ART. III
Only bishops and coadjutors can confer the Consolamentum.

ART. IV
All Pneumatics, Perfecti or SI can perform the Breaking of the Bread ritual.

ART. V
The Appareillamentum is the exclusive privilege of the patriarchal throne.

ART. VI
L'Initiation will publish these three rituals incessantly.

ART. VII
The Martinist Order is declared to be fundamentally Gnostic. All SI take rank in the class of Perfecti.

ART. VIII
The Gospel According to John is the only Gnostic gospel.

Issued in Paris under the seal of the Very High Gnostic Synod, the 28th day of the twelfth month of the restored Gnosis IV year.

+ The Gnostic Patriarch, Primate of the Albigeois, Bishop of Montsegur.
+ The Bishop of Toulouse.
+ The Bishop of Béziers.
+ The Sophial of Warsaw.
+ The coadjutor of His Grace the Patriarch, Bishop of Milan.
+The coadjutor of Toulouse, Bishop of Concorezzo.
+ The elected Bishop of Avignon.
By mandate of His Grace and the Very High Synod.

Deacon Referendum

EXECUTORY
The Holy Pleroma is invoked. We order this Decree of the Highest Synod executed in all assemblies.

Ϯ VALENTIN,
Gnostic patriarch,
Primate of the Albigeois, Bishop of Montségur.
(Published in *L'Initiation*, September 1893)

Gnostic Catechism

Published by mandate
of His Grace the Patriarch
and by order of the Very High Synod

Decree of the Very High Gnostic Synod for publication of the Catechism:

The Very High Gnostic Synod, reunited in Paris on the 10th day of the 7th month of the fifth year of the restoration of the Gnostic, states:

The Gnostic Catechism contains three parts and is preceded by the mandate of His Grace the Patriarch. It will be published unceasingly and throughout the Darkness of Kenoma. It is the will of the Holy Aeon.

By decree of the Very High Synod,   Imprimateur
The great referendum of the Seal,   ☦ Valentin
Bishop of Concorezzo and coadjutor
of the Bishop of Toulouse, Commander
of the Order of the Dove and the Paraclete

+Paul

INTRODUCTION

CHAPTER I

CONFESSION OF FAITH

Question: Are you a Gnostic?
Answer: Yes, I am a Gnostic.

Q: What is Gnosis?
A: Gnosis is illuminative science.

Q: What do you mean by that?
A: I mean the science of the divine, of the human and the natural, or the infinite with the finite.

Q: What is a Gnostic?
A: Someone with knowledge of the science of divine things.

Q: Is this science in opposition to faith?
A: Science is opposed to blind faith, but not to reflective, profound and reasoned faith.

Q: Is this definition contrary to the teachings of the apostles?
A: No, because Paul wanted the Corinthians to grow in faith, speech, science and goodwill. (2 Corinth 8,7)[5] and Peter adds faith to science (2 Peter 1,5).

---

5 Pistei kai logo kai gnôsei kai pasê spoudê.

Q: What do you conclude from this?
A: I conclude that a real Gnostic has "reasoned and
       scientific knowledge of the divine". which means
       knowledge of the absolute and the manifestation of the
       absolute.

Q: Can you recite the confession of faith?
A: I confess to the doctrine of Emanation and redemption
       through Gnosis.

Q: Does this confession, together with morals, provide
       redemption[6]?
A: Yes, through the grace of the Holy Aeon.

---

6 With redemption, we mean liberation from the domain of the Demiurge and
reintegration in Pleroma.

FIRST PART
ORIGINS

CHAPTER II

THE ORIGIN, OR SIMON MAGUS

Q: Tell us of the origins of Gnosis.

A: The truth is eternal, Gnosis came forth in time and space, in a concrete format. It followed the spiritual descent of Jesus, the flower of the very high Pleroma.

Q: Where and how?

A: In Samaria, after the descent, through the revelation of Simon Magus.

Q: Tell us of this great man.

A: The Magus of Samaria was the teacher of Gnosis and his teachings contain the seed of the most magnificent doctrine that is the Absolute's most illuminating expression.

Q: Did he create Gnosis?

A: No, it is the truth and is therefore uncreated, but he did unveil it.

Q: Was it unknown before he appeared?

A: Yes, in its Western form, but in the East it was taught in its hidden form. It is, was and will continue to be the mystical garment.

Q: Where was this Magus born?
A: In Gitta, Samaria.

Q: What name did this prophet have?
A: He had the name "the Great Virtue of God".

Q: Who assisted him?
A: A brilliant woman by the name Helena, whom he met in Tyre. He tore her from her vile life and delivered her from the tyranny of evil and connection to the fall.

Q: Was Simon a scientist?
A: Yes, he possessed Plato's science, the gift of the oratory and poetry. He had knowledge of anatomy. He discovered the law of blood circulation. Finally, he was a great theurgist and thaumaturge.

Q: Was that all?
A: He had a simple and just soul and an incontestable honesty.

Q: What was his view of the apostles?
A: He was already famous at the time the first Christians started their mission and he asked the deacon Phillip for baptism as a superior initiation.

Q: How do you explain his behaviour towards Peter?
A: When he wanted Peter to confer upon him the Holy Spirit by imposition of hands, he did not see any wrong in this. He did not offer him money to buy the Holy Spirit, as some malicious individuals stated, but he offered them the regular fee for initiation at that time.

He himself possessed the Spirit to an eminent degree.

Q: What did he say to Peter whom spoke ill of him?
A: He offered him the following words of goodness and humility: " Pray for me so that nothing of what you accuse me shall take place".

Q: What was Helena to Simon?
A: She was a symbol of suffering. A living picture of the fall of thought into matter. He loved her as nobly as a man such as he could.

Q: Was Helena worthy of his love?
A: Yes, without a doubt. She was worthy of it by her faith, her devotion, her brilliant intelligence and her attachment to the prophet.

Q: How did the Magus of Samaria die?
A: No one knows anything precisely about his death. The fables that are told about his life are of apocryphal origin. The origin of these fables and his ability to levitate come from narrow-minded and hateful Christians.

Q: Did Simon compose any works?
A: Yes, he wrote the *Antirrhetica* and *Apophasis Megale*.

CHAPTER III[7]

THE DOCTRINE OF SIMON MAGUS

Q: What does Simon's Gnosis try to explain?

A: Everything: God, man and the world. The trilogy of synthesis.

Q: What was there in the beginning?

A: Fire. Moses said that God is an all-consuming fire. This fire is very different from the elementary fire that is only its symbol. This fire has a more visible nature and a mysterious nature. This secret, occult nature conceals itself in its appearance. In the same fashion as its appearance conceals itself in the occult. The invisible is visible to the Spirit, but ignorant people cannot distinguish spirit from form when they do not know the law of correspondence.

Q: What would this fire be in idealistic philosophy?

A: The comprehensible and the sensible, power and action, idea and speech.

Q: What is matter?

A: It is the outward manifestation of the primordial fire.

Q: What is spirit?

A: It is the interior manifestation of the primordial fire.

---

7 To answer questions from our readers, we will say that the Catechism we publish today was found among Valentin II's (Jules Doinel) surviving papers. It is a fragmented work, which does not constitute a fully doctrinal work one can rely on. Footnote from the journal [La Gnose].

Q: Then what does this fire contain?

A: It contains the absolute and the relative, the informal
     and the formal, spirit and matter, the one and the many,
     God and the emanations of God.

Q: What can you conclude from this?

A: That this fire, the eternal cause, evolves through
     emanation, that it is in eternally becoming.
     Developing itself it is stable, permanent and remaining.
     It is the One that is, was and will be, immutable, infinite,
     absolute, substance.

Q: Why does it develop?

A: Even though it is unchangeable, it is not static. The
     infinite can act since it is intelligence and reason[8], as
     God passes from power to action.

Q: Explain this evolution.

A: Thought has an expression which is speech, the Word[9].
     So the ineffable is giving itself names, and by
     giving itself names it acts, evolves, emanates and moves.
     By expressing a thought, from this thought, they are
     bound together through sense. And from two comes
     one, just as one turns into two through emanation. This
     fire emanates through two, a couple, a Syzygy. In this
     couple, one is active and the other is passive, one is
     masculine and the other is feminine, one is he and the
     other is she. In Gnosis, this emanation of a pair is called
     the holy Aeons.

---

8 It can be active, even though it does not act, for the activity is neither latent nor
non-manifested.

9 Logos. RØ

Q: What are the names of the Aeons?
A: God emanated six Aeons:
Spirit and Thought (Νοῦς og Επινοια),
Voice and Name (Φωνη og Ονομα),
Afterthought and Reflection (Λογισμος og Ενθυμησις).
And God is fully present in each of the Aeons.

Q: What did the Aeons do?
A: To fulfill God, the Aeons emanated new beings. The
divine law of analogy dictated this. These pairs
therefore continued as masculine - feminine, active -
passive. It was the ladder of the Supreme Being that
Jacob saw in a dream while he slept with his head upon
the sacred stone Beth-El, under the starry skies of the
desert. The Aeons rose up and down the mystical
hierarchy in pairs. They form an unbroken chain that
winds its rings out in anabasis and katabasis, from God
to the world, from the world to God. They are a duality,
man and woman, a divine couple, angel-woman,
associated forms, united thoughts, they provide the
framework for matter and spirit, fulfilling God in that
which is and lead them back to God. The law, which
governs all, binds them and raises and lowers them, is
the primordial fire: It is love. Such is the first or the
divine world.

CHAPTER IV

THE CONTINUATION OF SIMON'S TEACHINS

Q: Tell us about the worlds in between.

A: They consist of six Aeons who reflect the six upper
     Aeons, and inhabit them. They have the same name.

Q: What does Simon call the second world?

A: Unimaginable air, the Unity, the Father lives here. It
     develops as the fire developed in the divine world. It
     manifests itself through its Thought, Epinoia. It is also
     called Silence.

Q: What happened?

A: Epinoia, the Aeon of the feminine silence, emanated
     angels and forces that turned into the third world; the
     world we live in. These angels wanted to keep it trapped,
     and this led to the fall and the need for redemption.

Q: Where does humanity come from?

A: Humanity comes from one of these angels, the
     Demiurge, the Jewish and Christian God.

Q: What happens with Epinoia?

A: Although she was held captive by the angels, she was
     brought back by her divine instinct, and she longed then
     even more strongly for Silence, the Father she had left.
     The angels kept her and inflicted sufferings on her. They
     locked her up in the human bodily prison. Thus began
     the divine exile, and her painful emigration and
     transmigration through the centuries. It is the fall of the

thought into matter, it is the fall, the primordial evil.

Q: What did this lead to?
A: All decay is in need of redemption. Epinoia
wanders through the ages, from woman to woman, as
a scent that moves from vase to vase. This is how Simon
met Helena; she was the incarnated thought, Ennoia.
He loved her, transformed her, rescued her, and used the
parable of the lamb that was lost and found.

Q: Summarize this.
A: When Simon saved Helena from deep depravity, the
Father sent the redeemer into the world in his spiritual
form, and redeemed Ennoia from the tyranny of the
criminal angels. In Judaea, he is called Jesus and the Son.
In Samaria he is called Simon and the Father. For future
people, he will be the Holy Spirit whom we await, God's
great virtue, the woman who is to come.

CHAPTER V

BASILIDES

Q: Who is the second mentor of gnosis?

A: It is the Syrian Basilides who taught in Alexandria in the 130's.

Q: Summarize his teachings.

A: His first principle is the pure being that is itself equal, the impalpable essence which is both spirit and matter at the same time. It is pure potential.

Q: What does he call it?

A: The incomprehensible Father, and he is found in three compounds: The Ogdoad, Hebdomad, Hyle or matter.

Q: What is the Ogdoad?

A: It is the divine world that is ruled by an executive archon[10].

Q: What is the Hebdomad?

A: It is the world in between, ruled by the second archon.

Q: What is Hyle?

A: It is the dark realm ruled by chaos.

---

10 Greek for ruler. RØ

Q: What do we call the unification of these three worlds?
A: Abraxas. It is a continuous series of 365 worlds or heavens[11].

Q: Explain evolution and involution.
A: God has spread out in diversity, and eventually rediscovers himself to lead everything back to the unity in himself. Man is the breakpoint between these movements

Q: How does redemption happen in the three worlds?
A: In the divine world Protos Christos, the executive archon's son, will redeem the Aeons.
In the world in between, Deuteros Christos redeems the spirits.
In the Hylic world man will be redeemed by the earthly Christos, who is the son of the Aeon Myriam.

Q: What is Jesus made of?
A: He is created by a secular body that comes from the hylic, a physic-body coming from the world in between, and a body that is spiritual or νους, which comes from the divine.

Q: Render for us the great words of Basilides.
A: "Jesus was the first fruit that came from the essence. He is the ideal that all true Gnostics seek, as he redeems by illumination."

---

11 You get 365 if you total the numerical value of the Greek letters that constitute the word or name Abraxas or Abrasax.

CHAPTER VI

VALENTINUS

Q: Who was Valentinus?

A: He was the third and greatest teacher of Gnosis. He was Simon Magus's successor in the patriarchal seat. He is the originator of our assembly and was the most harmonious and well-spoken of all the masters.

Q: What can you tell us about him?

A: His teaching, which is also our doctrine, will be explained later. We will now tell you about the person and his influence.

Q: Tell us about the person.

A: According to his opponent St. Epiphany, he was born in Egypt in the region Phténotite, and he participated in the Alexandrian schools. Here he learned Platonic metaphysics.

Q: What statements are there about him from the church fathers?

A: St. Jerome says that he was "highly educated" and the author of the *Dialogue against the Marcionites* considers him a superior consciousness[12]. Tertullian praises him for his deep knowledge of the theories of the great Plato. Clement of Alexandria treats him as a dangerous and formidable enemy.

---

12 Ουχ εντελης ανηρ.

Q: In what time period did Valentinus live?

A: The scholar Amélineau, who has provided many services to Gnostics, confirms that our famous mentor and father came to Rome between years 135 and 141 of the Christian era. He would have been around 40 years old at that time. He died at the age of 70, full of honour, virtue and wisdom.

Q: Where did Valentinus die?

A: On the island of Cyprus, between the years 160 and 170.

Q: Where did Valentinus serve as a mentor?

A: He taught in Alexandria, Rome and all of Egypt.

Q: What did Valentinus say?

A: He said he was the disciple of Theoden, who himself had been the disciple of the Apostle Paul. He had his teachings from the secret teaching that Jesus given to His Apostles.

Q: Which works did Valentinus leave behind?

A: *The letter to Agathopodus* of which we have fragments, homilies, a speech on friendship, psalms and a thesis on the origin of evil, of which Origen kept a well-spoken passage. His main work was entitled *Sophia*.

Q: Which writers wrote about Valentinus?

A: St. Irenaeus, Clement of Alexandria, Origen, Tertullian, Philastrius and Theodoret. It is also written about him in *Philosophumena* and in St. Epifanes's writings.

Q: Give us some quotes by our master.

A: "God was love, but love without someone to keep dear is no longer love. Therefore, he emanated a goal for his love."
This passage contains in itself the seed of the Gnostic doctrine *par excellence*, namely emanation.

Q: Continue.

A: "In the uncreated, everything coexisted. In that which has become, the feminine conveys substance while the masculine gives substance shape."

Q: Continue.

A: "The psychic man has partly strayed as he is under the influence of the demiurge."

Q: Can you give us the magnificent passage which Clement of Alexandria reproduced in his *Stromateis*?

A: "There is only one good being, and his power is realized through his only son. The heart is truly a palace inhabited by many impure spirits. The heart is a seedy inn, darkened by evil travellers who are demons. But when the Father, who is good arrives there, the heart is sanctified. The heart is enlightened by the goodwill of Pleroma which shines as a star. Happy is he who has such a heart, for he shall see God."

Q: Continue.

A: "After the creation of man, the Logos planted an angel-seed in his soul. This spiritual seed that Jesus, the flower of Pleroma, puts in the soul, prevents man from being destroyed."

Q: What conclusions do you draw from this?
A: That hylics will perish as immortality is conditional.

Q: Recite a passage from one of the homilies Valentinus gave to his disciples.
A: "From the beginning you have been immortal (απ'αβχης). You are children of the eternal life. If you had allowed death to enfold you in his realm, it would have been to annihilate and disintegrate it; to let it die in and through you. You dissolve the world but are not dissolved by it yourselves. You sovereign of all creation and destruction."

Q: To whom is this passage addressed?
A: It addresses the pneumatic and the elect.

Q: What did Valentinus call Gnosis?
A: The mystery which is hidden for centuries. To tear the veil and reveal the mystery, Jesus was born of the Virgin Miriam.

Q: According to Valentinus, what happiness will befall the pneumatics?
A: "They will live in the world of the Lord, the Ogdoad. The wedding of the Lamb will take place there. They will be engaged to angels, and love will last forever."

Q: Finish by reciting Valentinus' beautiful passage on
        evil for us.

A: "I cannot find the strength in me to say that God is the
        author and creator of evil. For who can nourish such
        thoughts about him? He is good and there is no evil in
        him. He wants those who seek him to be good as he is
        good. Evil had its origin in the hylic which was not
        created or formed, but distorted in chaos."

CHAPTER VII

THE GNOSTIC SCHOOLS

Q: Are there other Gnostic schools?

A: Yes.

Q: Name the most important ones.

A: The schools of the Samaritan Menander, Saturnilus from Antioch, Carpocrates and Marcellina, Marcion, Bardesanes from Syria and finally the school of Justin and the branches of Naazener and Ophite schools.

Q: What is the general theme which unites all these schools?

A: It is the vital doctrine of emanation.

Q: Does the Valentinians scold these schools?

A: No, he admires and honours them, as different aspects of the same truth.

Q: Is it so that all Gnostics are brethren?

A: Yes, all Gnostics are brethren, all agree on the same fundamental doctrine and confess the Holy Aeons.

Q: And you, what are you?

A: I am a Valentinian Gnostic. My father is Pleroma, Christos is my redeemer, Simon and Valentinus are my teachers, Helena and Sophia are my moral support, and I await the coming of Our Lady Pneuma Hagion, the eternal woman.

Q: Recite the Valentinian prayer.
A: *Beati vos, Aeones,*
Vera vita vividi,
Vos Emanationes
Pleromatis lucidi,
Adeste, Visiones,
Stolis albis candidi.[13]

Q: Recite the angel prayer.
A: *Ave candidum Lilium fulgidi semperque tranquilli*
Pleromatis,
Rosaque praefulgida coelicae amoenitatis,
de qua nasci et de cujus lacte pasci Jesus,
Flos Aeonum, voluit,
divinis infusionibus animos nostros pasce.
Amen.[14]

Q: Recite the prayer of Pneuma Hagions.
A: *Rorate, coeli, desuper et nubes pluant Justam.*
Rorate, coeli, desuper et nubes pluant Pulchram.
Rorate, coeli, desuper et nubes pluant Bonam.[15]

Q: To which church do you belong?

---

13 O, ye holy Aeons filled with true life. O, ye emanations, Pleroma fills you with light. Come, holy visions. In white and shiny garment.

14 Hail, shining white Lily of the gleaming and ever tranquil Pleroma, and ever brilliant Rose of celestial delightfulness, from whom is born and from whose milk is nourished Jesus, the Flower of the Aeons, who willed that our souls be nourished by the showers of thy divinity. Amen.

15 Let thy dew descend upon us, and may Justice rain from the clouds in heaven above. Let thy dew descend upon us, and may Beauty rain from the clouds in heaven above. Let thy dew descend upon us, and may Goodness rain from the clouds in heaven above.

A: The Holy Gnostic Assembly, led by the Holy Spirit who
       is feminine, ruled by the Superior patriarch and The
       Superior synod of bishops and sophials.

                                              VALENTIN II.

SECOND PART

THE DOCTRINE

We must remember that this Catechism is an unfinished work, and we publish it as it is.

The second part contains the exposition of the doctrine which was begun by S.G. Paul, bishop of Concorezzo, and stands unfinished. The following chapters are all that have been written. The third part, which would be about the church, was never begun. We believe it was preferable that we refrained from changing it or finishing it, as our thoughts cannot necessarily follow the mindset of the first authors.[16]

CHAPTER VIII

THE OGDOADE

Q: The clarity and purity of your answers has aroused
        interest and admiration. I researched and have become
        a disciple. I have gone from being a sceptic to become
        a devout listener. O initiate, I am waiting for the light
        that illuminates, if you will enlighten me.

A: A son of Seth will never be denied the Holy Gnosis.
        Direct your heart's attention to me, let the voices of
        the mind be quiet, listen with your soul; give yourself to
        me as a child in the arms of its mother; and may the
        Aeons give this unworthy mentor strength and goodness
        - I am ready for your questions.

---

16 Footnote from the journal La Gnose. The chapters that follow in this catechism was written by Paul Sédir (Yvon Le Loup), (N.D.E)

Q: What was in the beginning?

A: In the beginning slept Nothing. It is the Silence and it is the Abyss. It is insoluble, without action, without beginning and without end. It is alone, all-powerful, invisible, indescribable, such is the beginning.

Q: Explain this, please.

A: It is indescribable. It is what is inside and above knowledge; outside knowledge which can be sought, or the ability to know. It slumbers outside of what one can see, what we observe or see. However, it is in them, but has no characteristics. It is both in their appearance and outside it. It is the motionless engine. It knows neither pleasure nor pain, but it is the origin of them. It is the centrepiece, the eternal, and it is zero. It is the Silence and the Abyss.[17]

Q: What does this primordial essence contain?

A: Fire and light.

Q: What do you mean by fire?

A: Fire, the centre which evolves itself to become the circumference, it is a hard and violent creation, yet a dry and burning attraction. It is the eternal hunger and thirst of the abyss. It is dumb and has no true life, for when it radiates and absorbs at the same time, it cannot find success in places other than in the second principle which is light.

---

17 There seems to be a reflection here: Bythos, Abyss is masculine, and Sige, Silence, is feminine, but this depends on how one sees it.

Q: What do you mean by light?

A: The light is the absolute manifestation of life. It is formed
       by the lofty radiance of the fire which successfully
       overwhelms the attractive force of the light. It is the
       power from the living waters' impermeable love; the
       eternal mould which has given rise to everything that
       has been made. Fire and light have always existed, and
       maintain their individuality even though they keep each
       other in themselves.

Q: What is that which you call Aeons?

A: Aeons are the primordial creative power. These are the
       balancing forces emanating from the Origin.

Q: How do the Aeons come to be?

A: The Aeons come to be through the individualization
       of the constituents of the abyss. They form themselves
       through their own volition around the midpoint, so
       that they constantly receive a balanced overall impulse
       which is continued in the same harmonious way. The
       impulse then passes to the lower worlds.

Q: How do the Aeons emanate from the abyss?

A: Through *syzygies* or pairs. The feminine Aeons make
       the substance which is being simultaneously formed by
       the masculine Aeon.

Q: So what is the individual Aeon's property?

A: The property is persistence and immortality, for in the
       essence they are always themselves equally.

Q: What is the order of emanation?

A: In the beginning, the following Aeons were emanated from the Silence: The Abyss and the Thought – Bythos and Ennoia; then Spirit and Truth – Nous and Aletheia. This supreme fourfold manifested in Word and Life – Logos and Zoe; and in Man and Assembly – Anthropos and Ekklesia.[18]

Q: Can you reveal the nature of these beings to me?

A: I cannot, for your spirit is not yet strong enough to withstand this bright light, and the human words express the relationship between these absolute forces only poorly. Pray that the Aeons enlighten the eyes of your soul in your quiet contemplations. If the prayer is sincere enough and the desire big enough, they will answer you.

---

18 It is important to point out that there are different opinions on the order of these Aeons.

CHAPTER IX

DECADE

Q: Are the Aeons you have mentioned the only ones that
      exist?

A: No, in the holy Pleroma they constitute only the
      Ogdoad, the first diathesis of the absolute.

Q: How does the hierarchy of the Aeons continue?

A: With the Decade and the Dodecade.

Q: What is the Decade?

A: The Decade is the reunification of the five Syzygies
      which emanated from the Word and the Life, in
      thanksgiving to the Origin.

Q: Which Aeons constitute the Decade?

A: They are Bythos (Abyss), and Mixis (Mixture); Ageratos
      (Timeless), and Henosis (Union); Autopgyes (That
      which exists by itself) and Hedone (Pleasure); Akinetos
      (Immovable) and Synkrasis (Synthesis); Monogenes
      (the Only Begotten) and Makaria (Delight).

Q: What do these names represent?

A: These names represent the collective beings, the souls
      of life and the rays of the Abyss. They constitute the
      manifested power of Logos and Zoe. They indicate the
      qualities of Sige. You will see that their rays extend
      towards the boundaries of the void. They fill the three
      worlds with radiance, and in them and through them
      live all visible and invisible beings.

Q: So what are the properties of the Word?

A: The Word is the Father's only begotten Son. It was the
       first that existed in the void. "it was in God", which is
       why it will not age; "it is God", and therefore exists
       in itself. And finally "all beings came into being by him,
       and nothing came to being except through him".
       Therefore, it is also motionless.

Q: Explain the force of Life.

A: Since the Word is not in motion, Life manifests as
       motion. Zoe is therefore: Mixis and Synkrasis. Through
       her vast timeframe, she unites contradictions while
       she lets things become, according to the divine legality
       of harmony; pleasure and delight.

Q: What do the concepts of pleasure and delight mean?

A: They refer to the blooming, development and fulfilment
       of life, which comes from their harmonious and united
       forces. The pure love between man and woman has its
       fullness in the invisible, through the song which is sung
       about the struggle between their souls. So it is in all
       facets of life … Because "that which is below is like that
       which is above, and that which is above is like that which
       is below" (but in an opposite way).

CHAPTER X

DODECADE

Q: What is the Dodecade?

A: The Dodecade is the reunification of the Syzygy which emanated from Anthropos and Ekklesia, the last to be born of the heavenly Ogdoad.

Q: How many Aeons constitute the Dodecade?

A: The Dodecade is formed by twelve Aeons who emanated in pairs.

Q: Which are these Aeons?

A: They are called: Parakletos (the Merciful) and Pistis (Faith); Patrikos (Paternal) and Elpis (Hope); Metrikos (Maternal) and Agape (Love); Aeinous (that which is always prudent) and Synesis (Intelligence); Ekklesiastikos (that which unites the Assembly) and Makarides (perfect Joy); Theletes (Will) and Sophia (Wisdom).

Q: What is the role of these twelve Aeons?

A: They fulfill the recognition and description of the Father's powers, and so they complete the expression of the Absolute in Pleroma. Together with the Decade, they form the complete cycle from which all beings come. For they are 22, and 22 equals by gematria the 4 who generated them.

Q: Can you summarize everything you have just said
       about the Pleroma?

A: According to our Master Valentinus, Pleroma consists
       of the incomprehensible Father, and the thirty Aeons
       He emanated. The primordial essence contains the
       powers of the four qualities that are the four Aeons.
       These are realized in the second quaternary of the Divine
       Ogdoad. From this Ogdoad emanates all the other
       inhabitants of Pleroma. Therefore Pleroma is the being
       who opposes Kenoma, the void, and descends toward
       him by the will of the first Father.

       Now we will understand the continuation of involution.

CHAPTER XI

THE TEARS OF SOPHIA

Q: Please present the outer development of the creation.

A: Although the Aeons were similar to themselves, the wish for reunification with the primordial Father was greater, the further away in emanation they were. They wanted to reintegrate into the absolute being with whom they were no longer united.

Q: Was Pleroma prey to an inner turmoil?

A: No, turmoil could not occur in Pleroma. What you call turmoil is merely the tendency of contradictions between emanation and reintegration.

Q: Since Pleroma no longer exists alone, did it have to produce a form of disaster between the two powers?

A: The consequence or imbalance occurred as follows: When the mysterious Eogonie developed in the radiance of the Empyre, the powers of emanation weakened. Meanwhile, the desire for reintegration grew greater and greater in the hearts of the Aeons. There came a time when this desire was carried away by the radiance; it was at that moment Sophia started to act.

Q: Tell me about the Aeon Sophia.

A: Sophia is the limit of Pleroma. She is the body of Pleroma that gives it form. She is eternal and the origin of all beings and structures everything.

Q: What happened?

A: Sophia's desire for reintegration with the eternal Silence was stronger than the power of emanation. She knew the Abyss of the Origin and how the Aeons came to be, and she wanted to imitate this divine action.

Q: What did the desire of Sophia lead to?

A: Sophia succeeded only in creating a formless creature called Ektroma. When the Aeons saw this, they knelt before the Father and asked Him to redeem Sophia.

Q: What are the other names of Ektroma?

A: Enthymesis or Sofia-Achamot.

Q: What did the Primordial Essence do?

A: He took pity on the unhappy Aeon, and emanated a new pair as a clear example of integrity. This he did through the second Syzygy – Nous and Alethia.

Q: What were the powers of this new Syzygy?

A: They were called Christos and Pneuma Hagion, Christos and our Lady the Holy Spirit.

Q: What did these Aeons do?

A: They started separating the pure from the impure.

Q: How did they proceed?

A: The Father of all fathers created Horos to this effect, the important and active Aeon of Boundaries. Armed with a sword he stands by the limit of Pleroma, and with an unfailing vigilance, he keeps out everything that cannot pass.

Q: What did Ektroma become?

A: This did not happen before Elektroma was perfected. She was named Ogdoad[19] or the Exterior Sophia. Christos and Pneuma Hagios then ascended into Pleroma. Their return restored the peace and harmony of the Empyre.

Q: How did the Aeons express their joy?

A: In the recognition of the Origin, they wanted to give him an Aeon who was a perfect representation of the unity and harmony that from then on reigned in Pleroma.

Q: Which Aeon was this?

A: His was the Aeon Jesus, formed by the purest essence of each of the Aeons. He is the crown of the divine emanation, "the Flower of Pleroma", the greatest pontiff.

Q: What happened to Sophia?

A: When she saw that Christos and Pneuma Hagion were leaving her, the Ogdoad felt abandoned. She directed her prayers and needs towards them and the Aeons in Pleroma. And they sent the Aeon Jesus to redeem her.

Q: What did Jesus do for Sophia-Achamot?

A: He neutralized her feelings, feelings of fear, grief, anxiety, agitation and supplication. He turned them into permanent plastic essences.

---

19 This Ogdoad should not be confused with the one described in chapter VIII.

Q: How did Jesus transform the sorrows of Sophia?

A: From fear he made the psychic essence. From grief he made the essence of matter which is the essence of demons. And from the supplication he made the path that leads to repentance and the power of the psychic essence. This is the path of the Demiurge or the right-hand essence.

Q: Do these three essences have any other names?

A: The psychic essence is also called the "Heavenly Place", the Hebdomad. This is the domain of the Demiurge. The essence of matter is also called hylic or diabolic, and the daemonic essence is called spiritual or pneumatic.

Q: What happened next to the Ogdoad?

A: Sofia was brought back to her mate, Jesus, after having been comforted. Together, they recreated the emanations of Pleroma in the Ogdoad, the heavenly Jerusalem.

CHAPTER XII

THE DEMIURGE

Q: What is the Demiurge?

A: The Demiurge is the son of Sophia, created by her movement towards the light. He is the prince of psychic essence, the one who unconsciously performs his mother's will. He reigns over the Hebdomad.

Q: What is the work of the Demiurge?

A: it is to shape the exterior world we live in. The world that was created in the beginning from the three essences, from Sophia's fear, grief and anxiety.

Q: What did the Demiurge create?

A: He created all beings that have the same essence as him, called right-hand beings. He also created those who are shaped by matter and are called left-hand beings.

Q: Of whom is the Demiurge an image?

A: He is the inverted image of Monogenes of Pleroma, because "that which is above is like that which is below, but turned upside down".

Q: Through what process did he create the world?

A: He first took the two essences hylic and psychic. Then he created that which is on the left and the right side, the heavy and the light; that which pulls up and that which drags down. He included all beings in the seven worlds of the Hebdomad.

Q: From what elements were these pulled?
A: The raw material the Demiurge used in his work was the emotions Sophia-Achamot created.

Q: Specify these.
A: From the fear Sophia felt, he created the spiritual substance of the beings of the world. From the sadness he created all the evils of the world. From the anxiety and confusion he created physical things.

Q: How did the four elements come to be?
A: The Demiurge took earth from the densified bewilderment, water from Sophia's tears, air from her overall grief, and finally fire from the origin or root of these three sufferings.

T PAUL

This catechism was published in number 1 (Nov. 1909), 2, 4 6, 7, 8 (June 1910) by the journal La Gnose (N.D.E).

ORGANIZATION OG SACRAMENTS

THE STRUCTURE OF THE CHURCH

The church was constructed as a hierarchy with a patriarch as the temporal head, mundane because Ennoia or Sophia-Achamot was considered the spiritual head of the church. The patriarch was the secret successor of the apostle John, and was also the one who fulfilled all the ordinations.

The patriarch signed with Ϯ, a double tau that is a Greek letter. The patriarch was addressed as *Your Highness*.

The patriarch also had a council. This council was called The Superior Synod. From this unit the church was managed and guidelines issued (such as the texts in Decree –and catechism in this book).

Otherwise, the church was managed by bishops and sophials who were awarded their respective dioceses. There were also bishops and sophials who served as Deputy heads of diocese, and these received the title coadjutor.

The intention was that all dioceses was to be led by a bishop and a sophial, who would as such be the earthly manifestation of a pleromatic pair, a Syzygy.

The bishops and sophials were elected in an assembly of church followers, deacons and deaconesses. The regalia of the office was a silver ring decorated with an amethyst. This was worn on the right hand. The bishops and the sophials chose an alias, a Gnostic name, for their office. They signed with this name and a simple tau: T.

The bishops and sophials were addressed as lord or lady.

In the diocese they could have many congregations, however they worked as administrators of the sacraments at the place in which they lived. The place where the congregation gathered was the church's operational unit. Here, the sacraments were administered and the teachings conveyed to the assembly. The congregation was led by a deacon or a deaconess who had been ordained by a bishop or a sophial. The church members were those who had received the Consolamentum and had thus become perfecti.

The Consolamentum was mainly administered by bishops and sophials, but could just as well be performed by deacons and deaconesses in their absence.

THE SACRAMENTS OF THE CHURCH

Doinel was inspired by Simon Magus and Valentinian theology and this gave the church its content. The aesthetics and expressions of the church, however, were mainly taken from the history and form of the Cathars. The Église Gnostique had three sacraments, and in addition, they had ordinations. The importance of the ordinations will not be described further here, as they are the church's way of empowering perfecti to Episcopal ministry, or to appoint a deacon or deaconess. The three sacraments are Consolamentum, The Breaking of Bread and Appareillamentum. Consolamentum and Appareillamentum have both taken their names from the Cathar tradition.

Beyond this, dreams and visions were important, and as Ennoia was the spiritual head of the church, communication with her could happen through transes or dreams at night. This was, however, not a sacrament as such, but an integral part of the spiritual practice in the Église Gnostique, and this was not just reserved to Doinel. The communion with Pleroma, or the fullness, was integrated in the members' practice, and was as such associated with the actual experience of Gnosis in everyday life.

Consolamentum

Consolamentum was the fire - or spiritual baptism of the Cathar church which is also described in the New Testament. The purpose of the sacrament was, and also is in the Église Gnostique, to transfer The Holy Spirit to the initiate. It wiped out all so-called sin, abolished the effect of the fall and transformed the recipient into the new or restored man.

The consolidated person became a perfecti, a walking angel upon earth, who was only separated from the divine by a thin veil. It is not known how old this ritual is, but it might have survived from earlier Valentinian Gnostic sources. The Cathars claimed it originated from Christ himself.

An important difference from how the Cathars used the sacrament was that one could receive Consolamentum several times in the Église Gnostique. Furthermore, it was not associated with a strict ascetic lifestyle. The reason why it was given several times was that this would strengthen the effect in the receiver. However, it was expected that the lifestyle would be characterized by a persistent reverence for The Holy Spirit who had united with the perfecti.

Consolamentum marked that one had become a full member of the church, and in the Cathar tradition as well as in Doinel's church, this required extensive preparations through counseling, self reflection and training. For the Cathars, this was something that happened in the assembly of believers in the form of religious education that resembled the education the early church gave to its graduates.

The Église Gnostique, however, was a church with members who carried with them experiences from other societies in France. Most of them were Freemasons and Theosophists, and many belonged to Rosicrucian, Kabbalistic or Hermetic orders.

Thus, one could say that much of the preparation work of becoming a spiritually oriented person was methodically and systematically addressed by other institutions before the person came to the church. This arrangement became more formalized with time, and in the beginning of the nineteen hundreds, the Gnostic church had formally become what it had always been, "the church of the initiates".

The Breaking of Bread

The Breaking of Bread naturally originates from Jesus's Last Supper, where he says that his followers should do this in remembrance of him.
The Gospel of Mark 14, 22-25:

> "And as they did eat, Jesus took bread, and blessed, and brake it, and gave to them and said, Take, eat: this is my body.
> And he took the cup, and when he had given thanks, he gave it to them: and they all drank of it.
> And he said unto them, This is my blood of the new testament, which is shed for many.
> Verily I say unto you, I will drink no more of the fruit of the vine, until that day that I drink it new in the kingdom of God".

The Cathars had other perspectives of this sacrament than the Catholic Church with its theory of the bread and wine's actual transformation into Jesus's body and blood. The Cathars' considerations may appear somewhat closer to the Protestant theory, where the blessings of the items made it so one could realize Christ in oneself. The Cathars underlying theological reason for this was that the bread and everything made in the world is made by Satan, and therefore is not suitable as the spiritual vessel.

Based on Doinel's Breaking of the Bread, it seems that he has continued this approach, as it appears more as a memorial than a spiritual transformation formula.

Appareillamentum

In the Cathar church, this sacrament was a form of public rite of confession, which society participated in on a monthly basis. The confession led to various forms of penance that could vary from prayer sessions to periods of fasting. There is disagreement on whether the whole society participated in this sacrament or whether it was reserved to the perfecti.

In the Église Gnostique this is also a form of confessional rite, but it is a general confession of being "guilty and fallen as my mother Sophia-Achamot". Furthermore, the recipient of the sacrament says that: "I will deny the works of the Demiurge and pray for forgiveness". Here, it is more a metaphysical confession of an innate state of being in the world, and that this has led to certain negative consequences. One has not come to confess the specific deeds, but to deny the Demiurge. One has come to be redeemed from that which is between one's current way of life and the life or existence which is fullness (Pleroma). In a Gnostic spirit, this is to a greater extent about a profound shift in perspective rather than becoming something new. Man is considered good, but has strayed into the spiritual psychosis of the Demiurge. This has clouded the understanding of self and human thinking.

In response to this, the patriarch gives the percipient an angel, a guardian angel. And since he has already found his way back to his divine nature through Consolamentum, he is now reinstalled in Pleroma, the Gnostic heaven, by being united with the angel so that they again constitute the divine pair, the Syzygy.

It is important to understand that these are mystical images that reflect an inner experiential process.

Through the sacraments, man becomes again what he was in the beginning: pleromatic man. This also has many other Gnostic consequences which will not be discussed further in this book; this is however the main theme in one of my previous books: "*The Key. Sethian Gnosticism in the postmodern world.*"

Consecration of bishops

This is the sacrament that conferred on a man or a woman the powers and capacities needed to become the leader of a geographic jurisdiction. The text uses the term bishop. However it is most probable the same formula is used with women when consecrated sophial.

The next part of the book will present the actual sacraments of the church.

Consolamentum

The bishop is seated behind a table with a white cloth. On the table is the Gospel of St. John between two candlesticks. The deacon and deaconess are seated on each side of the episcopal throne.

The male perfecti stands adjacent to the left of the table, the female on the right. The men have a white belt around the waist and the women a white veil over their heads and faces.

Those who are receiving the sacrament are kneeling in front of the first row, each with a burning candle.

The assembly rises when the bishop enters, and recites the Valentinian hymn.

Beati, vos Æones
Vera vita vividi;
Vos Emanationes
Pleromatis lucidi;
Adeste visiones
Stolis albis candidi.

The deacon then reads the first verse of the Gospel of St. John, first in Greek, then in their mother tongue.

En arkhei en ho logos, kai ho logos en pros ton theon, kai theos en ho logos. Houtos en en arkhei pros ton theon. Panta di autou egeneto, kai khoris autou egeneto oude hen ho gegonen. En autoi zoe en, kai hê zoe en to phos ton anthropon; kai to phos en tei skotiai phainei, kai he skotia auto ou katelaben.

In the beginning was the Word, and the Word was with God, and the Word was God. The same was in the beginning with God. All things were made by him, and without him was not anything made that was made. In him was life; and the life was the light of men. And the light shineth in the darkness; and the darkness comprehended it not.

The bishop delivers his homily.

The choir intones the Pater Noster:

Pater hemon ho en tois ouranois:
Hagiastheto to onoma sou;
Eltheto he basileia sou;
Genetheto to thelema sou,
Hos en ouranoi kai epi ges;
Ton arton hemon ton epiousion dos hemin semeron;
Kai aphes hemin ta opheilemata hemon,
Hos kai hemeis aphekamen tois opheiletais hemon;
Kai me eisenenkeis hemas eis peirasmon,
Alla hrusai hemas apo tou ponerou.
Hoti sou estin he basileia,
Kai he dynamis, kai he doxa,
Eis tous aionas. Amen.

The congregation answers: "Amen".

The deacon and deaconess lift up the candles from the altar, and place themselves on either side of the bishop.

The bishop takes off his right glove, and goes forward to those who will receive Consolamentum.

The candidates extinguish the candles and continue to kneel with their hands together.

The women who will receive Consolamentum lift their veils.

The bishop places his hand on the head of each of them as he says:

Memor esto verbi tui, servo (servæ) tuo (tuæ), in qui mihi spem dedisti. Hæc me consolata est in humilitate mea.

The candidate answers: "Amen".

The bishop kisses him or her on the forehead and says: "Osculetur me osculo oris sui."

When the bishop has returned to his seat, the choir sings the hymn of Consolamentum.

Consolemini!
Consolemini!
Popule meus.
Consoletur me misericordia tua!

Lucerna Pleromatis
Lucet meis semitis.
Inclinavi cor meum
Ad tuum eloquium
Consoletur me misericordia tua!

Eructabunt labia mea hymnum.
Concupivi salutare tuum.

Attolite portas, Æones, vestras!
Et elevamini portæ Pleromatis!
Consoletur me misericordia tua!
Amen.

The bishop rises, the assembly kneels, whilst the deacon and deaconess raise the candles, The bishop administers the Gnostic blessing, and says:

Consoletur vos Sanctissimum Pleroma, Æon Christos, Æon Sophia et Æon Pneuma-Hagion!

The choir answers: "Amen".

As the bishop retires, the choir sings:

Domina, salvam fac Ecclesiam,
et exaudi nos in die qua invocaverimus te.
Domina, salvum fac Patriarcam nostrum Valentinum,
et exaudi nos in die qua invocaverimus te !
Domina, salvos fac Episcopos
et exaudi nos in die qua invocaverimus te.

BREAKING OF THE BREAD

The Gospel of St. John is placed between two candlesticks on a table dressed with a linen cloth. The bishop, deacon and deaconess are standing in front of the table.

The prelate wears the stole (when the patriarch performs the ritual, he uses the superior pallium).

The perfecti who are participating, gather. The women are covered with a white veil, and the men have a white belt around their waist. They kneel to receive the blessing from the bishop.

After the blessing, they stand up and the choir sings:

Beati, vos Æones
Vera vita vividi;
Vos Emanationes
Pleromatis lucidi;
Adeste visiones
Stolis albis candidi.

When the hymn is over, the bishop recites Pater Noster in Greek:

Pater hemon ho en tois ouranois:
Hagiastheto to onoma sou;
Eltheto he basileia sou;
Genetheto to thelema sou,
Hos en ouranoi kai epi ges;
Ton arton hemon ton epiousion dos hemin semeron;
Kai aphes hemin ta opheilemata hemon,
Hos kai hemeis aphekamen tois opheiletais hemon;
Kai me eisenenkeis hemas eis peirasmon,
Alla hrusai hemas apo tou ponerou.

Hoti sou estin he basileia,
Kai he dynamis, kai he doxa,
Eis tous aionas. Amen.

Congregation answers: "Amen".

The deacon presents the chalice and the bread to the bishop,
who lays his hands on them and says:

Eon Jesus priusquam pateretur mystice,
accepit panem et vinum in sanctas
et venerabiles manus suas, et,
elevatis oculis in cælum, fregit (the bishop breaks the bread),
benedixit (the bishop draws a tau over the bread and wine),
et dedit discipulis suis, dicens (everyone bows):
Accipite et manducate et bibite omnes!

The deacon carries the paten and the deaconess the chalice, and
they display the elements for the perfecti.

The organ plays a slow religious march.

The bishop lifts up the bread in front of the congregation and
says:
"This is the spiritual body of Christ."

He puts the bread back on the paten, kneels and prays.

He rises, lifts up the chalice and says:
Calix meus inebrians quam præclarus est!
- Calicem Salutaris accipiam et nomen Domini invocabo.
This is the spiritual body of Christ.

He kneels and prays.

He rises, breaks off a piece of Jesus's spiritual body and eats it,
then drinks of the blood.

Pause. The organ plays.

He then goes to the perfecti, giving each of them bread and wine.

Silence. The organ plays during the prayer.

Back at the altar, the bishop raises his hands and says:
May the holy blessing of Pleroma always be with you.

The rest of the blessed bread is burnt, see that the body of the
Lord is not desecrated.
After this, the bishop administers the Gnostic blessing and
withdraws with the two assistants on either side. They each take
their candle with them when they leave.

APPAREILLAMENTUM

This sacrament can only be transmitted by the patriarch. The candidate has to turn to him with his request in a separate letter with the following formulation:
"In dignity I, (name), ask to receive the holy Appareillamentum". The request is sent to the diocesan bishop or sophias for approval. The patriarch will inform the seeker of the time and place for the ritual.
Appareillamentum cannot be transmitted to a pneumatic who has not received Consolamentum at least once. On the chosen day, the candidate meets in the chapel. He is dressed in black, with his head bare and his hands tied together with a white cord. Appareillamentum is never given with others present. The Patriarch and the candidate are alone.

The candidate kneels and says:
I come from Pneuma-Hagion, guilty and fallen as my mother Sophia-Achamot. I have come to deny the work of the Demiurge, and ask for forgiveness from the holy Aeons through you, your holiness.

The patriarch, who is dressed in the superior pallium, puts his hands on the candidate's head and says:
Remittuntur tibi peccata tua quæ sunt peccata mundi.
Amen.

He then puts the right corner of the pallium on the head of the candidate and says:

Our Lady Sofia, Our Lady of The Holy Spirit, Our Lady Hedone, remember your servant who denies the Demiurge, his thought and works. Give him a guardian from the Aeons, who will redeem him forever. Amen.

The patriarch can then put the candidate's hands in his and impart some words in confidence. He then loosens the cord and says:
The Aeons solves it in Pleroma as I resolve it in Kenoma and the third world of the void. By Helena-Ennoia, by Hedone and by Sofia you have support: They are with you!

Receive the mystical kiss.
The patriarch kisses the candidate on the forehead, the kisses in the form of a Tau.

The candidate kneels lower, recites the opening verses from the Gospel of John:
"In the beginning was the Word, and the Word was with God, and the Word was God. The same was in the beginning with God. All things were made by him; and without him was not any thing made that was made.
In him was life; and the life was the light of men.
And the light shineth in darkness; and the darkness comprehended it not".

Then he rises he says:
God is love!

He bows to the patriarch and leaves the chapel in silence. The patriarch remains alone in the chapel in silent worship for 15 minutes.

Consecration of bishops

The ordination of a new bishop takes place in the assembly of perfecti.

The patriarch, assisted by two coordinators, asks the acceding bishop the following questions:

1.. Do you believe in the most holy Gnosis?
2. Do you accept the two fundamental doctrines of the Gnosis?
3. Do you accept the appointment and the responsibility involved?

After confirming this, the acceding bishop sits himself on a chair in front of the patriarch's seat. The deacon lights the two white candles. The patriarch and the two coordinators withdraws, led by the deacon who carries the double Tau.
The acceding bishop meditates and mentally prays, while the deaconess opens the Gospel of St. John and places salt, oil and insignias on the table.

The choir, accompanied by the organ, sings the psalm Dixit Dominus Dominae meae, sede a dextris meis:

Dixit Dominus Domino meo sede a dextris meis
donec ponam inimicos tuos scabillum pedum tuorum
virgam fortitudinis tuae emittet Dominus ex Sion
dominare in medio inimicorum tuorum
populi tui spontanei erunt in die fortitudinis tuae
in montibus sanctis quasi de vulva orietur tibi ros
adulescentiae tuae iuravit Dominus
et non paenitebit eum tu es sacerdos

in aeternum secundum ordinem Melchisedech
Dominus ad dexteram tuam percussit
in die furoris sui reges
iudicabit in gentibus implebit valles
percutiet caput in terra multa
de torrente in via bibet propterea exaltabit caput.

Those who will perform the ordination return, and the acceding bishop kneels in front of the patriarch.

The patriarch recites the following prayer:

Domine-Domina, Dea-Deus, benedicere digneris huic electo episcopo N. et gregi quae ei committitur. Per Helenam Dominam Nostram Amen.

The first coordinator recites Pater Noster in Greek.

Pater hemon ho en tois ouranois:
Hagiastheto to onoma sou;
Eltheto he basileia sou;
Genetheto to thelema sou,
Hos en ouranoi kai epi ges;
Ton arton hemon ton epiousion dos hemin semeron;
Kai aphes hemin ta opheilemata hemon,
Hos kai hemeis aphekamen tois opheiletais hemon;
Kai me eisenenkeis hemas eis peirasmon,
Alla hrusai hemas apo tou ponerou.
Hoti sou estin he basileia,
Kai he dynamis, kai he doxa,
Eis tous aionas. Amen.

The second coordinator recites the introduction to the Gnostic Gospel.

In the beginning was the Word, and the Word was with God, and the Word was God. The same was in the beginning with God. All things were made by him, and without him was not anything made that was made. In him was life; and the life was the light of men. And the light shineth in the darkness; and the darkness comprehended it not.

Then the three ordaining bishops put their hands on the head of the acceding bishop, one by one, and says:
"Electe episcope N. ego, auctoritate O Eonum, te sacro, te consacro, te creo et te confirmo episcopum N. (names diocese)".
They embrace him.

They anoint him with the blessed oil in the shape of a Tau on the forehead while they say: "Pleroma te sanctifice!"; on the lips while they say: "Pleroma te amplificet!"; and on the heart while the say: "Pleroma te magnificat!".
They place a few grains of salt on his tongue and say:
"Vos estis sal terrae. Quod si sal evanuerit, in quo salietur!"
They place a candle in his right hand and say:
"Vos estis lumen mundi."
They give him a cup of water and say:
"Vos estis fons aquae salientis in vitam aeternam."
After this, the ones ordaining sit down and the acceding bishop kneels in front of them.

He places his hands in theirs and takes the oath:
I swear between your venerable hands, by the mighty name of the most holy Pleroma, faithfully to fulfill my obligations as bishop of (name of place). May Sophia and all the Aeons support me.
All answer: "Sic! Amen!"
The patriarch blesses the new bishop and gives him his Episcopal

insignia: A Tau in purple ribbon, purple gloves, infula and the Episcopal ring.

He then delivers his homily.

He administers the patriarchal blessing.

He presents the new bishop to the perfecti by saying: "I proclaim N, bishop of N".
The congregation answer: "Fiat! Fiat!".

The congregation kneels to receive the blessing from the new bishop, and finally all come forward and kiss his ring.

The Knights of the Paraclet dove

The Église Gnostique was not the only Gnostic organistation Doinel established. To follow the Gnostic church, he founded an order of knights which he called the *Order of faydit[20] knights of the Dove and the Paraclete, L'ordre des chevaliers faydits de la Colombe du Paraclet.* This order was founded in 1893. However, this order was not inspired by the Freemasonic order of knights who flourished at that time, such as the Freemasonic Templars and the Knights of the Holy Grail, but was an independent expression.

The purpose of the order was to link the restored Gnosticism together with the chivalric Albigensianism from the twelfth century. It would further tie well-educated men and women to the Valentinian church via an exterior organization.

Doinel's intention was to form a sort of honorary guard protecting the Gnosis, which is called the Gnostic Mystery.

He therefore recruited educated and renowned people, so that the order would be able to spread the Gnostic message in the circles and saloons the members frequented.

The order, like the church, was closely linked to Doinel's understanding of Gnostic tradition.

According to Doinel, Helena was the inspiration behind the organization. It is unclear if he is referring to Helena as a spiritual entity or as an individual.

---

20 Faydee was a landowner who had lost his area because of his affiliation to Catharism.

Degrees, regalia and organization

The order was established with three degrees, as well as the office of the Grand Master that belonged to the patriarch. These three were the Commander, Knight and Baccalaureus.

These three groups also had correspondence to the Valentinian classification of the human development as hylic, psychic and pneumatic.

Moreover, this had implications on how Doinel considered Freemasonry. The symbolic degrees corresponded with the hylics, for they had much to learn here. The psychics corresponded with the high-degrees, and especially the Scottish Rite with its 33 degrees, while the class of pneumatics corresponded with the Gnostic doctrine or Gnosis

The ribbons of the order, which were used in all the degrees, were blue and decorated with a dove flying downward. The Dove of the Order referred to the Paraclete, who is described as the Aeon Pneumia-Hagion, the feminine aspect of the Gnostic system.

The ribbon of the Grand Master was the patriarchal pallium with a silk embroidered dove. Next to the Grand Master there was a Grand Mistress with the title Esclarmonde. This was in memory of the Cathar Duchess of Foix.

The Commanders, who were the bishops, had a four fingers wide sash. The Dove was attached to a white satin rosette where the sash crossed by the left hip.

The Knights had a two fingers wide ribbon around their neck, and this amounted to a neck adornment.

The Baccalaureus had a ribbon in the size of an honorary legion. This was attached to the buttonhole in the suit.

The Commanderies, which were the order units, should according to Doinel have been established in Albigensia, Aquitaine, Burgundy, Ile de France, Slavia, Albion, Languedoc,

Italy, Spain, Flanders, Normandy and Britannia. Together, these twelve symbolized the holy communion of Christ.

At the superior Synod meeting in September in 1894, the bishops wrote a draft for the constitution of the order. This was not completed, and the order was probably continued as a formality related to the Episcopate. The bishops who have continued the Église Gnostique, has also decided to sign with the title Commander of the Dove and Paraclete, to continue the tradition of the order.

ADMISSION AND CEREMONIES

The bishops were naturally recruited through their ordination, and were as such closely related to the order operation from the beginning. It is also possible that they were automatically admitted when they were consecrated bishops.

The knights of the order recruited from amongst those who were initiated into the Gnostic schools, the Martinist Order or Kabbalistic societies.

The Baccalaureus, which consisted of outer circle of adherents, were not required to take any oath or vow, and were not obliged to belong to the Valentinian doctrine or the Église Gnostique.

The admission to the Knighthood followed a classical formula for knighting, and incorporated both men and women. In this admission ceremony they swore, amongst other things, an oath condemning Simon Montort and the crusades in southern France. In doing this, the order carried with it the memory of the massacre of the Cathars carried out at the behest of the Catholic Church.

The knighting formula used was as follows: "In the name of St. John and the martyrs, I knight you. Be faithful, loyal and pure!". The martyrs to which this formula refers were the Albigenesian knights, perfecti and deacons, those who died on the battlefield in the south of France or who were executed by the inquisition. The martyrology of the order was recited in memorials and contained names such as Guilhabert de Castres, Pons d'Adhémar, Esclamonde de Foix, Roger de Foix, Raymond de Toulouse, Correti de Languedoc, etc.

The martyrology was reportedly based on *Fonds Doat*, containing over five hundred Cathar names.

The word of the order was Montségur, which refers to the known Cathar castle where the last major resistance movement had fortified themselves, and the password of the knights was *"ad spiritum, per Helenam!"*, a password that clearly linked the order to the Gnostic tradition of the Église Gnostique.

HOMILIES AND ARTICLES

Regarding the selected texts

This part of the book consists of some articles written by Jules Doinel. He wrote several articles, most of them within the categories Gnosticism, Freemasonry, poetry and the history of religion.

As this is a book on the Église Gnostique, the criterion for the material chosen for this volume is that it is connected to his Gnostic authorship. Furthermore I want to give a broad picture of Doinel as a Gnostic teacher.

It is also my intention to give the readers of this book some understanding of the teachings presented to the congregation. There are however other texts referred to in the articles in this book that are omitted. The main reason for this is that the texts are lost, unavailable or their content is already covered in the present material.

GNOSTIC STUDIES: SIMON MAGUS

Translated into English by Thomas Williams in February, 1890

The Magus of Samaria is the first doctor of the Gnosis. His teaching contains the germ of that grand philosophy which we, towards the end of this nineteenth century, after an eclipse of several hundred years, recognize as the most perfect and luminous expression of the absolute.

I say an eclipse, but in reality the Gnosis has never been without its disciples and its apostles. Both, through persecution and what is even worse, ridicule, have been obliged to protect themselves by maintaining an inviolable silence, wrapped in the obscurity of uncomprehended symbols.

A sovereign interest draws us towards the high priest of Samaria. Not that he has invented the Gnosis, for it was taught under another form in the temples of Egypt, in India and Chaldea, the Gnosis being in fact as old as the Truth, of which it is the mystic garment. But Simon was the first to draw up its dogmas in their esoteric shape, and he is, as his name indicates, the ancestor, the first parent of the Gnosis posterior to Jesus Christ.

He was born at Gitta in Samaria, which, proud of his celebrity, called him the Great Virtue of God. After having lived at Tyre, where he met Helen, his lovely and mysterious companion, he went to Rome and for a time rivalled the renown of the Apostle Peter.

Simon was deeply versed in Oriental and Greek culture. Empedocles and Stesechorus were known to him, and he also was imbued with the ideal philosophy of Plato. A contemporary of Philo the Jew, he had frequented the school of Theosophy at Alexandria. He knew anatomy, having written a celebrated treatise on the circulation of the blood and the physical system of the female body. He was equally well grounded in practical Theurgy[21]. Magus, writer, physiologist, mathematician and orator, this great man was cut out for the performance of some special mission.

Already celebrated in the early days of Christianity, Simon devoted to the service of the Gnosis a soul grandly simple and single-minded and of the purest honesty.

Many even of his enemies have been obliged to acknowledge this, and M. Amélineau proves this to be the case in his book on "Gnosticisme Égyptien". Simon, being present at the wonders worked by the deacon Philip, asked to be baptized. Like all Initiates, he only saw in this ceremony a form of initiation.

He in no wise pretended to turn from the Gnosis.

In the request he made to Peter to confer upon him the Holy Ghost by the placing of hands, he never recognized a departure from his original principles. Nor did he offer money to buy the Holy Ghost, as the ignorant and the malicious say, but simply the customary and legal price of initiatory societies for the possession of the symbolical degree, which he wished to obtain. A European adept would act in a precisely similar manner, if he wished to be admitted to mysteries which were still unknown to him. In the division which subsequently took place between the apostles and the magi, the former were in the wrong, and Simon gives a touching example of his humility and gentleness in the words he addressed to the dark and bigoted Cephas: "Pray for me, so that nothing of that which you predict for me may happen".

Tradition says that Simon of Gittha made the acquaintance of Helen in a brothel; that he reclaimed her and placed her amongst the initiated. But there is a great deal more than this meant by the tradition, for she was to him the symbol and living image of

---

21 Divine magic with the aim of deifying man.

the fall of thought into matter. Nobly as was possible to such a man, did he love this woman, and she requited his love with marvellous intelligence and profound affection for him.

We know nothing as to his death. The fables which are told concerning his end being apocryphal inventions of narrow-minded Christians, based on the theurgical power of levitation often possessed by theosophical adepts.

Simon wrote the "Anthiretica: and the Great Apophasis of which the author of "Philosophumena" has preserved some fragments. By the aid of these we may obtain a fairly correct idea of the doctrine of the Samaritan doctor. The Gnosis claims to explain everything. It is active in every department of human thought, being equally concerned with that which belongs to heaven as with that which is of the earth.

The Gnosis, as its name shows, is Knowledge. God, man, the world, are the trinity of which it is the grand synthesis.

Simon Magus places Fire at the beginning, Fire having been the first cause of the cosmos. God, says the initiate Moses, is a consuming fire. This fire, very different from the earthly fire which is merely its symbol, has a visible and a hidden existence. Its occult and secret essence hides itself behind its material manifestation or visible appearance; which latter again withdraws itself into its hidden essence. In other words, the invisible is visible to the initiate while the visible is invisible to the profane, which means that the profane are unable to recognize the spirit, disguised under its outward form: the Vedas taught in earlier times this original dogma when they treated of Agni, the supreme fire. This fire of Simon is the same as that of Empedocles; it is that of the fire-worshippers of Iran. It is the burning thicket of Genesis. It represents the Intelligible and the Sensible of the divine Plato, the Power and the Act of the profound Aristotle; and it is also the flaming star of the Masonic Lodges.

In the external manifestation of the primordial fire we have all the seeds of matter, while its interior manifestation evolves the world of spirit. So that this fire containing the absolute and the relative, matter and spirit, is at once multiple and one, or God and that which emanates from God. This fire, the eternal cause of all, expands by emanation. It is eternally becoming. But while developing, it itself remains stable and permanent. It is in fact that which is, has been, and shall be, the immovable, the infinite, the substance of all.

But while thus immutable it is not inert. The Infinite may act because it is intelligence and reason. From the potential it passes to the active, and thought becomes an expression: the word. Thus Intelligence becomes aware of itself and by so doing acts, evolves, emanates. In formulating its thought, Intelligence unites the moments of this thought and binds its ideas one to another by the tie of reason, and as two come from one, because one in emanating must become two, fire emanates by couples, of which one is active, the other passive, one male, the other female, one he and one she. The Gnosis calls this two-fold emanation the Eons. Thus the sphere of the absolute, the superior world, was peopled by six Eons, or six first emanations from God. Simon called them Nous and Ennoïa (spirit and thought), Phone and Onoma (the word and the name), Logismos and Enthumêsis (reasoning and reflection), and in each of these six emanations is God in a potential state.

"In each of these roots", said the Sage, "the Infinite Power was in its entirety. It had to be formulated by a shape in order that it might appear in all its essence, virtue, grandeur, and effects so that the emanations would become equal to the infinite and eternal Power. If on the other hand it were not to be manifested by a form, the Power could not become active and would be lost for want of being used; just as a man who having an aptitude for grammar and geometry, if it is not used obtains no sort of benefit from it and it becomes lost to him and he is just as if he had never had those powers."

By this Simon meant that the Eons in order to be God-like must create. So that just as God passed from the potential to the active state, so the Eons must do likewise. And this is required by the divine law of analogy, and thus the six first emanations became the cause of six new emanations.

The Syzygies, like the six first, continued to emanate male and female, active and passive entities. " It is written", says Simon, "that there are two kinds of Eons having neither beginning nor end and issuing from one common root, the Silence (the great Sige) which is the invisible and incomprehensible power." One of these seems superior to the other; it is the great Power characterized as the Intelligence of all things; it orders everything and is male and positive, the other is inferior and is called the great Thought or female Eon. These two Eons are complementary and manifest between them the middle region, the incomprehensible air which has had neither beginning nor end.

See what a wonderful picture is presented to us in the divine ladder which Jacob saw in a dream as he slept with his head pillowed on the sacred stone of Bethel beneath the starry firmament which spanned the Desert. The Eons mount and descend this most mysterious ladder in pairs and constitute the links in the chain which stretches from God to Earth and back again to God, and each two are male and female, associated forms or united thoughts. They weave the woof of spirit and of matter, realizing God in things and carrying these back again into God, and the law which knits and directs them elevates and abases them and works as the sacred and primordial fire which, as God, is infinite and absolute and as expressing which in its highest expression may be called Love.

Next Simon opens to us the second world. It is peopled by six Eons, the reflection of the first six and bearing the same names. The incomprehensible air or second world is inhabited by the Father, He who is, was and shall be, without beginning or end, male and female living in one unity. He develops in the same way as the fire of the first world, for He manifests by the power of thought. The Father, which is the Power, and the thought which it produces, are complementary, being in reality one, as represented in the male which envelopes the female, the Spirit in the idea, or Nous in the Epinoïa. In other words, the Spirit has a thought which it proclaims by the word or the name Father. This Father is also Σιγή or silence.

Epinoia, the female Eon, enticed by love, leaves the Father and emanates angels and powers from which proceed the world which we live in. These angels, forgetting the existence of the Father, have wished to keep amongst themselves Epinoïa, and from this cause we have their fall and the necessity for a redemption.

Man is the product of one of these angels, the Demiurgus, which the Bible calls God. By him man is made double, after his own image and appearance. The image is the spirit which circles the waters of the abyss of which Genesis speaks.

Spiritus Dei ferebatur super aqua.[22] Man is an Eon, because in him there is the likeness of the Father, and like the Father, he will produce other beings. He will in fact reproduce himself.

This brings us to the anthropological doctrine of the Samaritan Magus. Fire is the principle of the act of generation, for to desire

---

22 From the Vulgata "And the spirit of God was hovering over the surface of the waters".

to be united to a woman is called "to be on fire" (πυροῦσθαι). This fire is one in itself but double in its effects. Man transmits in the seed the hot red blood, while the woman becomes the laboratory where the blood is turned into milk. It was thus that the sword of Fire which flashed before the gates of Eden in the hands of the Archangel typified by the quivering of its living flame the transformation of blood into seed and milk. Without this circulation of blood the tree of Life would die and the icy hand of death would congeal the World.

Continuing his subtle and profound analysis, Simon explained the development of the foetus after its conception.

Interpreting the words addressed to Jeremiah, "I have formed thee in the bosom of thy mother", he explained that man in Eden meant the foetus in the matrix, and he saw in the four rivers which fertilized the terrestrial paradise the ducts which adhere to the child and bring him nourishment.

How strange and original a conception of a great mind is this inspiration of genius drawn from the physiological meditations of a superior man in a primitive age. Let us now return to Epinoïa which the Angels, the ancestors of man, have retained captive. The Power of Thought drawn backwards by its celestial instincts is ever sighing after Sige and striving to return to the Father. The Angels hold it fast, however, and make it suffer that they may keep it amongst them, and finally they succeed in imprisoning it in a human body. This is the commencement of that long pilgrimage which the divine exile makes through a series of transmigrations and long ages of suffering. This fall of Intellect into matter is the origin of evil. It is forfeiture and to such there must be redemption; Enoia transmigrates from woman to woman through the ages like a scent which passes from vase to vase. The day on which Simon penetrated into the syrien den he met the migratory "thought" in the form of this Helen, of this prostitute whom he loved and whom he transfigured by his love. Loving her he applied with practical exactness the parable of the lamb who was lost and found. Thus runs the allegory. Just as Simon saved Helen from final degradation in taking her from the slough into which she had fallen, the Saviour sent by the Father descended to the world and delivered Thought from the tyranny of the lower Angels. In order to accomplish this act of infinite love Soter, the Saviour, the Son left the One, the Silence, the Fire, and passed through the first world down to the second where he incarnated in the world of Bodies, burying himself in the Astral Form or Perisprit. In Judea he was called the Son. In Samaria the Samaritans called him the Father. With the Gentiles he was the Holy Ghost. He was in fact the Great Virtue of God and Simon Magus knew himself in Him.

Just as Simon set himself to seek Helen, so the Saviour seeks the human Soul. He found her in a house of ill-fame, that is to say in Evil, and as Simon married Helen so the Saviour married the Soul.

"In truth", says the wise Amélineau, "this myth of Epinoia is very beautiful. The divine Thought held in bondage by inferior beings who owe it their very life and who wish to become its equal; degraded by these Angels and debased to the lowest degree, it forms a sublime allegory of the futile efforts of the human soul struggling towards God, of which it is the image, and falling from one abyss to another, from crime to crime, held in control by jealous spirits who, full of envy, endeavour to impede its upward progress towards him whom it resembles ".

Each one of us, for we are Eons, may become the Simon to a Helen or, reversing the parts, a Helen to a Simon. In order to fulfil our mission of Saviour, we, the initiates of the Gnosis, must appear to the profane as similar in form to them but their superior in spirit. Simon and Helen have taught us, and we in our turn must teach, the liberating power of the Gnosis, the illuminating science, the law or the lost Word of the Rosicrucians[23]. We will deliver our brothers and our sisters from the yoke of ignorance and superstition, of gross materialism and haughty scepticism. We will dress them in the white robes of Initiation. No matter where the seed is sown, so long as it is sown; saved by the Gnosis we become saviours, happy if we possess, perhaps not the genius of Simon Magus, but his great heart and wide charity.

Jules Doinel
(*Revue Theosophique*, February 1890)

---

23 Refers to the Rose-Croix degree in the *Ancient and Accepted Scottish rite*.

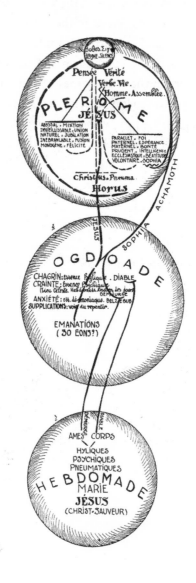

The spiritual world of Valentinus, drawn by Fabre des Essarts

THE VALENTINIAN GNOSTICISM

By Jules Doinel

To my brothers and sisters in the Gnostic church who are scattered in the hylic darkness of the world.

I

I am going to discuss the theme of Valentinian Gnosticism. It is an accomplished Gnosis, and I am approaching it with confidence, enthusiasm and trepidation. The reason for this is that I think it is time for the long suppressed, secluded and persecuted doctrine to promote its blessed and liberating lucidity to humanity now, at the end of this century.

I give thanks to Papus for allowing *l'Initiation* to receive this Gnostic message. It is not long until I openly will be able to publish the gospel that martyrs, apostles, masters and initiates lived, fought, suffered and cried for. With the help of the holy aeons, I will publish this to all upright people in the great and venerable city of Paris.

A gospel that has cost blood, from the time of Simon Magus to the Honorable Albigensians.

Our time is indeed privileged. It is witness to Kabbalism, theosophy, initiation, astrology and the renaissance of the hidden science. It contributes to a unique awakening. A whole constellation of elevated spirits shining on the psychic sky.

Magazines, papers and books light the candle from the orient for our Western world. The absolute emerges. Is it not correct that Gnosticism, which shone for centuries and almost died out, also resurrecting the firmament of the soul?

I am but a proclaiming voice, a voice who will not echo in the desert. May all profane disappear. We do not cast Ophir pearls for ignorant hylics.

II

The principles of Gnosticism are as follows:
The absolute emanates divine powers which are their nature. These emanations come in pairs, Syzygies, and are organized hierarchically top – down. They are aeons.

In the beginning was Silence, the eternal Aeon who gave rise to all aeons.
It was called the invisible silence, nameless, the unimaginable, the abyss and in everyday language God.
Principle and sense, eternity, was engulfed in itself without acting. In its unbroken silence, there were, however, two generators; the masculine and the feminine principle. One, the masculine, the one who enlightens from above. The other, the feminine, the one who enlightens from below. These two principles contained in them the root or origin of existence; or they were themselves the root or origin.
The Abyss (Buthor) engulfed itself and contemplated itself with its eternal wife, Thought (Ennoia).
Ennoia was also silent as he was, and she received the emanation's fruitful divine seed in the inexpressible embrace. It was through Ennoia that the Abyss would produce, for it was love, and love longs for growth. There is no love that does not desire something it may cherish.

III

The Abyss would therefore evolve, and through Thought it emanated Intelligence, the Aeon Nous, who was the firstborn (Monogenes). This was the only one who had the capacity to understand the scope of its dream. This was the first Aeon, it was masculine, and through him, God is revealed. The action which emanated him also emanated his partner at the same time. She was absolute Truth (Aletheia), the feminine Aeon who was with the masculine Aeon, subjectivity next to objectivity. This is how the first Tetrad came to be.

1-2. Sige – Ennoia (Silence and Thought).
3-4. Nous – Aletheia (Intelligence and Truth).
This first tetrad is the inner realization of the absolute. The Aeons who emanated from God, emanated as God. Nous and Aletheia made Speech and Life (Logos and Zoe). Logos and Zoe emanated Human Essence (Anthropos) and Assembly (Ecclesia). It is important to understand that Anthropos is man and humanity is but a pale copy of it, and that Ecclesia constitutes the entire cosmos. The masculine Anthropos and the feminine Ecclesia are the two archetypes that are in the world of intelligence and matter. These were the second tetrad.
5-6. Logos – Zoe.
7-8. Anthropos – Ecclesia.
The first and the second tetrad constitute the Ogdoad that are densifying the unimaginable beauty of the One in the absolute.

IV

The Aeons wanted to emanate in pairs, as Syzygies, such as the Father had done, as masculine and feminine principles. Logos and Zoe, therefore, emanated and brought forth:

· 1-2. Bythios og Mixis.
· 3-4. Ageratos og Henosis.
· 5-6. Autophyes og Hedone.
· 7-8. Akinetos og Synkrasis.
· 9-10. Menogenes og Makana.

These ten aeons constituted the Decade.

Anthropos and Ecclesia emanated and brought forth:

· 1-2. Paraclutos og Pistis.
· 3-4. Patricos og Elpis.
· 5-6. Metricos og Agape.
· 7-8. Aeinous og Sunesis.
· 9-10. Ecclesiasticos og Makarides.
· 11-12. Teletos og Sophia.

These twelve aeons constituted the Dodecade.

The reunification of the Ogdoad, Decade and Dodecade realizes the absolute in descending order. They constitute the Fullness, called Pleroma in Valentinian terminology.

Each of the Aeons is an apparition of the life of the divine Abyss. They recreate this together with a mystical chain to rise to his level. The Ogdoad is the higher level of the Dodecade, and the Decade is under this.

Valentinus agreed with Paul: "For in it dwelleth all the fullness of the Godhead bodily" (Col. 2, 9).

These concepts are the core of the great Valentinus's theology. We will now present the cosmogony of this Gnostic master in the same simple and unpretentious manner.

V

None of the Aeons who emanated out from the abyss knew their own essence or nature. The only one who knew this was Nous (Intelligence), who had come out of it, and his Syzygy Ennoia. Matthew and Luke says that "All things are delivered unto me of my Father: and no man knoweth the Son, but the Father" (Matt 11, 27 and Luke 10, 22).

It was this perfect science that was the objective of the Aeons. They emanated from God, they longed for him, they loved him, and they were consumed by an insatiable desire to know him. Nous would have communicated this perfect science to them had the eternal Silence allowed it. However, it was not allowed.

While the emanation continued, and the emanated Aeons moved away from the source, from the halls of the endless, the ignorance of the unfathomable mysteries grew bigger. Their insatiable thirst turned to suffering. Sophia experienced this suffering as encompassing. She was the last Aeon of the Dodecade, and the farthest away from the Father. Therefore, she was also the one with the poorest knowledge to her own secretive nature.

Although she was united with Theleos (Will), she could not maintain her masculine principle. She thirsted for the Abyss. She wanted to be one with him. She loved the source of emanation, the Father of the Aeons, the first Aeon. She struggled with the impossible. And in the fierce heat of this struggle, she would have become lost in the void, if Sige (The Father) had not set the Boundaries, the Horos-Aeon.

Horos got back within her the boundary. He was emanated to restore the harmony of Pleroma, and was concerned over Sophia's weariness. Horos felt impotent to fulfill his mission, for Sophia had already risen up in the fullness because of her infinite love.

Horos needed help. Therefore, Nous emanated a new pair:

Christos and Pneuma (Spirit).

These two Aeons were to silence the divine world Pleroma. Christos came to the Aeons and explained the extension of the Absolute to them, its laws, regulations, requirements and standards. Thanks to him, the Aeons understood that the absolute and unfathomable could only be recognized and comprehended through its manifestations, emanations and becoming, and that its indescribable essence rested in the eternal Sige (Silence).

After Christos, Pneuma spoke to the Aeons and taught them holy rest and the peace in holy unison.

VI

Sophia's weariness was not neutralized. In a state of violent desire, she gave birth through herself, without her partner Will. A feminine Aeon came out of her desire and united with the Abyss. This Aeon, who was Achamot, or the earthly Sophia, was torn out of Pleroma as soon as she was born, and into an exile of chaos. Here she wandered outside the boundaries of the divine world, blocked by Horos.

While Achamot fell from Pleroma, she had a brief revelation of the divine world, and this filled her with bliss. The feeling from the fall and the isolation pursued her in her exile. These beautiful verses from the esoteric poet Lamartine could have been intended for her:

> All mundane life was like exile from Eden,
> When God expelled her from the heavenly garden.
> The eye could see the fateful limitation,
> By the forbidden door, where she sat and wept.
> By the immortal break she could hear from above,
> A harmonious sigh of infinite love.

This unfortunate emanation often threw herself against the boundaries of the fullness, but Horos threw her back, as the archangel with the flaming sword cast Adam and Eve out of the mighty doors of Paradise.

Achamoth twisted around in the void and screamed:

> Limited in nature, banned from what I desire, mankind
> remembers heaven as a fallen god on earth.

From these holy tears, the moist element came to be, and matter was made by her immense grief.

Horos took mercy on Achamot. He emanated the Jesus – Aeon as a relief, so that she became his companion, and he made a reflection of Pleroma that shone on her.

When Achamot had been redeemed and restored in this way, she emanated three elements; the pneumatic, the psychic and the hylic. And from these three elements she formed the Demiurge, who in his unconsciousness was to possess the lower world.

VII

The Demiurge had a reflection of Pleroma and a natural element in him. He proceeded to part the hylic principle from the psychic, which from the beginning had been unbalanced in chaos. He then created six ruling powers by six Aeons. These six worlds are the heavenly spheres, the sixfold regions of the firmament.

The Demiurge organized the world through the hylic principle. Valentinus said: "This world exists in God, as a stain on a white tunic". The Aeon of this world is Satan, whom St. Paul also calls the ruler of this world. Satan is born through matter, as are the evil spirits who are his followers.

After a short while, the Demiurge wanted to fight Satan's malice. He chose man as the opponent. The soul of man is formed from a ray from the psychic principle, and the body was formed from a fragment of matter form the hylic. Then Achamot brought the pneumatic seed into him. This is the reason for the threefold nature of man.

The Demiurge was jealous of his own creation when he saw that man was ennobled with a pneumatic seed, with a spark from Pleroma.

To take revenge on man, he forced it to refrain from the redeeming fruit from the Tree of Knowledge, of good and of evil. Man broke this regulation and rebelled against the Demiurge, and this led to man being driven out from paradise. A threefold hylic cloth poisoned the soul of man. The Demiurge then left man to the hunger of the senses, and introduced it to pleasures that would strangle the seed of light within it; the seed of light which was the pneumatic clarity it had received from Achamot.

The good-hearted and soft, faint and motherly Achamot, the salt of the earth and the light of the world, gave man Grace, the invisible helper, who supports it in the opposition to the lower sexual desire.

Man is divided into three classes:

• Pneumatics or Gnostics, higher spirits or initiates, who follow the light of Achamot.

• Psychics who float between light and darkness, between Achamot and the Demiurge.

• Hylics who are loyal to Satan, and their souls are matter and will consequently be destroyed.

Seth, Abel and Cain represent these three categories.

VIII

The Valentinian redemption still remains.

Our world, the world of man, was redeemed by the Jesus Aeon. He came through the perfect channel, the Aeon we call Mary. The Jesus Aeon is not material. He is formed by a psychic principle he borrowed from the Demiurge, and a spiritual body. Jesus was activated by Christos who left Pleroma to rest in him. It was Christos who gave him perfect mastery over Satan's world. His teachings have redeemed and proceed to redeem pneumatics. Under the passion, he maintained and protected the impregnable Aeon Christos. The cross (Stauros) became the dividing line between pneumatics and other people, and so became a holy symbol for Gnosis.

This is in its entirety the teachings of Valentinus. The answers to all challenges. The absolute never appeared as bright as in this admirable story, which happens successively in the three worlds. The question of Gnostic morality remains. It is fitting to say that it advocates the innocence of God regarding evil, sorrow and injustice.

The origin of evil will be a subject for later investigations.[24]

May the Aeon who follows each and every one of us enlighten, illumine and cleanse us.

Jules Stany Doinel
(*L'Initiation*, April 1890)

---

24 This text does unfortunately not exist as far as I know. RØ.

THE FIRST HOMILY
On the Holy Spirit

To the Church of the Paraclete

I

The name of the Holy Gnosis is forgotten. Gnosis is the tragic story of the spirits fall into matter, and the arduous and necessary journey that the spirit undertakes from the emptiness of night (Kenoma) to the clarity of the divine Pleroma. A journey from the illusions and distorted images of matter to the domain of pure ideas and blessed peace; from the unfathomable abyss to the universal language of thought.

The philosophers called it the absolute, as an expression for incomparable truth, and the people called it God.

In order to make this journey, this turning back, the odyssey of the human spirit, the soul has two wings, namely science and love. They are the heavenly Christ and the Holy Spirit (Christos and Pneuma-Hagion).

II

These ways of speaking will not shake the idealists or make the indifferent smile. For centuries, the soul has been breaking this bread and drinking this wine. While materialists only relate to the parts, Gnosis can be rendered through the words of Jean Scot Erigène: "The danger lies not in searching for the nature of God with the torch of Logos, but to insist on being inside the limits of nature when driven towards the point where you have to break through."

Scot would have said this after relying on two sources to Gnosis, namely pure reason and vision. Gnostics are however far from those who despise experimental science.

They think as Plotinus and the authors of the Upanishads that above the sphere that constitutes the world of phenomena, the world of Maya, there is an incomprehensive sphere that the lower senses cannot comprehend.

They know that an idea that manifests itself is a theophany, a divine appearance in the human soul; and God as he manifests...

III

Gnosis is the field of knowledge of theophany, and the divine appearance. It is the science of aeons, the glorious theophanies, the reality of divine perfection.

The Lord's open eyes over the deserts' shadow gaze;
The air, earth, sea which the spirits have fertilized;
Angels with all names; mystic phantoms,
As the invisible world, more saturated than atoms;
The holy legions of the Father, who are in all places,
Who glows in the flames, and in wind and blown,
bear vitnes , invisible, to our earthly hate.

Lamartine

The great Emmanuel Kant once compared the soul who towers about the absolute with a dove who soars above eternity. However, Gnosis teaches and shows us that the absolute is where the soul moves, since the soul is an emanation of the absolute.

Ephrem from Syria said the gnosis wore a crown for those who loved it, and let them sit on a throne.

When the Lord said: "I will send the Paraclete to you to teach you all things", he announced both the Christian gnosis and the arrival of the Holy Spirit.

The prophetic voice of Jesus, he who is the flower of the Aeons, was forever answered by initiators and evangelical messengers.

When you browse through the Biblical apocrypha, you will almost incessantly hear the crying of the dove of the Holy Gnosis, and you will hear her cry out to people who hunger and thirst for justification and truth.

IV

John revealed to us that the Logos had emanated from God in the beginning, and that truth and life had emanated from Logos. John also revealed to us, through his prophecies, the new Jerusalem which descended from the heart of God; revered as a lady reveres her husband. This is the holy Gnosis. It is also he who sees the symbolic lady descend from heaven, clothed in the sun and crowned with twelve stars, with the moon under her feet. It is he who in the last chapter shouts out to the man in the name of the Lady:

"Amen! Come. Lord Jesus, come!".

It is Paul who speaks to the Colossians about the mystery of God. The mystery that is revealed in Christos, which has all the treasures of hypergenos in it. And in the letter to the Galatians, he says: "If you are accompanied by the Spirit, you are not subject to the law".

It is Apollo, in the admirable letter to the Hebrews, who presents the Son to us, monogenes who shall inherit everything and who God created the Aeons with. The only begotten, the glory of all and the image of divine substance, who sustains everything through Logos.

V

The teachers and bishops of Gnosis are carriers of the esoteric meaning of the Bible. The angels have entrusted us the pontiffs in the order of Melchizedek, the breastplate carrying the Urim and Thummin (3 Mos 8,8).

It is we who read from the book of the Law (Neh 8,8). What we have written is sealed with the king's name, and it is we who carry the king's ring (Est 8,8)

Is the following written about us?

> Who are those who are dressed in white, and where do they come from? They are those who have undergone great trials and have washed their robes in the spiritual blood of the Lamb (the ram), and are untouched by the transgressions of the hylic world.

"Gnosis is the core of Christianity" (the Duke of Adhémar. *Revue Théosophique*, 21st of June 1889). Here, my friends, is the most upright description of Gnosticism. Here, Christianity tells us whence we came and to where we are going. *Unde venis et quò vadis?*

To know this is all one needs to know. *Porro unum est necessarium!* This Gnosis of realization is the gem of the gospel. And it is for this gem man must sell and give away everything he has.

"Where do you come from, my soul?" asked St. Basil. "Who gave you a corpse to carry? Are you of heavenly origin, my soul you must teach me."

And the Gnosis answered: "You will realize all if you contemplate the Pleroma."

VI

The Honourable Mr. Franck pointed out that Gnosis expresses being as a complete and absolute summary of all systems of beliefs and ideas that mankind needs to realize its origin; the past and demise of mankind, its nature, non-existing paradox and challenges of life (*Journal des Savants*).

The first principle is the Abyss, the perfect unity which exists through itself, the incomprehensible Father. This principle cannot be defined as it is inscrutable. This is the being that has all possibilities in itself, enclosed by its own mystical silence (Sige). In itself, it has light, life, love and conciousness.

Should the unimaginable Father rise out of the silence if the abyss were flooded, and the powers in it processed itself, it would be love, and not desire, that governed it. And there is no love without something to hold dear.

From this unity comes duality (the dyad), a living duality, a theophany from the absolute, masculine and feminine, lover and loved; and that which is revealed as spirit and truth (Nous and Aletheia).

VII

We will end here, dear friends, and entrust the further spiritual history of development to the second Episcopal homily[25]. We leave this introduction to the divine manifestation to your mediations and contemplations.

You who partake in the church of the Paraclete, commune with your brothers through prayers and studies, through your attentiveness to the invisible shepherds, through your struggle with your own selfish ambitions and everything that can destroy generosity, and you will succeed in establishing a strong foundation for the society of pneumatics which the high

---

25 This text has probably been lost.RØ.

presence has proclaimed and promised us. Amen.

Given under Tau, 18th of August 1890, in Our Lady the Holy
Spirit's ninth year.

T Jules, Gnostic bishop

(Jules Doinel)

L'Initiation, September 1890

THE GNOSIS OF LOVE

I

To the Honorable Gnostic Synod.

My gentlemen and my brothers.

By looking at the Valentinian system we have seen that Sophia-Achamoth's exile from Pleroma was the origin of grief in the world.

However, what Valentinus is not telling us is that the aeons did not want to leave this infinite grief in the finite, and therefore asked the Abyss to send her a Paraclete. The Paraclete was worshipped by the Greek under the name Eros, and by the Aryans under the name Kama. The Paraclete is the eternal Eros, and he was formed by the union between the Abyss and the Silence (Bythos and Sige).

Eros was created through their union. In this way, the redemption of Sophia-Achamoth was accomplished through two parallel paths: the path of the Flesh and the Spirit. Jesus, the flower of Pleroma, regained spirit, for redemption is through Gnosis, not faith.

Eros received the flesh. Knowledge and love set in motion the great work that would happen in time and space.

Achamoth had a duplex spouse, her heart's spouse. It is this divine mystery we will explain.

II

Those who consider Achamoth a fable, are wrong and deceive themselves. She is an essence: The divine essence.

Her joys and sorrows are real. She embraces both sorrow and joy. She suffers and rejoices in us, in the spiritual. As her, we also are fallen, and like her, we will reintegrate back to the Fullness. So she is very important to us. Her story is also our story. She is the heroine in a tragedy that is staged by our blood and our tears. Valentinus, who first told this story, could not describe or understand all the consequences of the esoteric doctrine he himself had established.

And if he could have described and understood, he could not describe a being who was so close to the Apostolic on one hand, and paganism on the other. When he still says that love cannot exist without something to hold dear, he shows us that what is held dear, Achamoth, will be the subject for this love.

Valentinus has himself, through reincarnations, been present under other names, and was now to complete the miraculous work he had begun.

III

Before all early teaching, I put the premise and the rule of the holy Gnosis. Redemption is done by realization, not through faith. Faith without Gnosis is nothing.

Outside of Gnosis there is no redemption. However, the wise has experienced that Gnosis develops in love. Love is like a tawny eagle flying to its lover and leading him in to the atrium of Hedone, or lust's.

Let us no longer consider gnosis as something deplorable. She is cheerful and strong. She knows and she desires. She loves and enjoys loving. A Catholic mystery expresses this clearly:

Love triumphs.

Love rejoices.

Love rejoices in God.

St. John says, with the voice of the archangel, and cries from the island of Patmos: "God is love". Augustine of Hippo adds: "*Ama et qvod vis*[26]", and finally Sophia herself says: *"Omnia munda mundis*[27]".

Let us take a look at Sophia-Achamoth as she comes into being, from the divine Sophia in the world between. She becomes the victim of a cruel and spiritual anxiety where she is tormented in darkness, in the thick and demonic darkness the gospel simply describes as the outer darkness.

Those who consider Achamoth a fable, are wrong and they deceive themselves. She is an essence: The divine essence.

Her joys and sorrows are real. She includes sorrow and joy. She suffers and rejoices in us, in the spiritual. Like her, we also are fallen, and like her, we will reintegrate back to the Fullness.

So she is very important to us. Her story is also our story. She is the heroine in a tragedy that is staged by our blood and our tears.

IV

Through her terrible suffering, a strong prayer rose up from the Aeons, *omnipotentia supplex*, up to the Abyss. In an instant, Eros came to be. In an instant Abyss and Silence united. In an instant a ray sprang through the darkness, and Achamoth felt her loved one's heart beat in her own broken heart, the Sacred Heart.

The Song of Solomon is a pale reflection of the wedding hymn the Aeons sang. Eros incarnated and lived with us. The great mystical word was spoken: I.N.R.I.

Modern Rosicrucians overlook the deep meaning and beauty in this. Tau took shape. Rosecrucianism was incorporated, and the holy exchange took place.

Sons of the spirit and of the flesh, we are the children of Eros and Achamoth, and their union was declared insoluble from

---

26 Love, and do as you will.

27 For the pure, all things are clean.

Pleroma who blessed them, and this is blessing us through them. The Mother begins her ministry. The work of the Demiurge has sown burning embers. This is the fire Simon Magus describes in *Apophasis Megale*.

This fire has a dual nature; it is matter without spirit and spiritual without matter. Fire was worshipped by the Aryan and Persians, and the sun is its cosmic symbol: I.N.R.I. *Igne Natura Renovatur Integra*.

V

Here we can imagine a sharp and astute protest when the theologians of the Demiurge say: "Fire is lust." Let us then answer them clearly: "This fire is love." And let us be even clearer, and add: "This fire is a love in its fullest form, not divided, not superfluous, not pure lust as with the heathens, not sterile chastity as with the ascetics. It is the love that occurs when the spirit draws through the body, as sunbeams make crystals shine."

Let us continue. All Gnosis teaches us that the sexes co-exist in God, as man and woman. All Gnosticism conveys that the Aeons emanated in pairs, in Syzygies. The Father of the Aeons is androgynous, God-Goddess, and is called Abyss-Silence. All that emanates is like him. I have written the following in my Gnostic hymn in *l'Etoile*:

The Aeons emanated,
emanated in a row,
One and two are love's
unfathomable mystery.

Eros is holding Achamoth and the spiritual people; holding and loving men and women. The Aeon Hedone is the link. Desire is holy, and self-control is sacred, for neither the desire nor the self-control lead astray. They are love.

143

VI

That which distinguishes love from her fallen sister is corruption. Corruption does not love and does not look for anything else other than pleasure.

Corruption has pleasure as its objective, whilst for love pleasure is a means. This is the main and most important difference between them. One must be blind not to distinguish the one from the other. Gossip cannot stick on this diamond. Gnostic love is a relief, a wing that lifts us up to knowledge, to Gnosis. Two holding each other's hands and rising towards the light without ever returning back to the darkness.

O mother Achamoth, released by Eros, we recognize that we are her children and followers. We also recognize that we have come to be in her image and likeness. It appears that her will was to give us an example, by giving life to Simon and Helena whose history we know.

Famous lovers through the passage of night and sources of light: Simon and Helena! Abelard and Heloise! Dante and Beatrice!

– *quasi scintillæ in arudineo discurrunt!*[28]

They lit our way. They walked in front of us as our predecessors, as ancient runners, described by Lucretius. When they ran past, they gave us the torch of love – *et quasi cursores vitce lampada tradunt.*[29]

J.S. Doinel
l'Initiation, June 1893

---

28 Flying like embers through straw.

29 and the torch carrier's lives

GNOSIS OF THE SERPENTINES-NAASSENES

I

The Hebrew word Nahash means serpent. Naassenes took their name from this, and is usually described as serpentines (Ophites).

The author of *Philosophumea* indicated that they boasted that only they had delved into the Abyss, which meant that it was only they who knew it.

Their doctrine contained a deep and strong symbolism. The ideal man and the ideal man's son were their archetypal patterns. This man, who was both male and female (androgynous), carried the mystical name Adam. A beautiful passage from one of their hymns has been preserved: "From thee, emanates the Father (fatherhood), and with thee is the Mother (motherhood). Glory be to their immortal names. The Father of the Aeons (or better, the origin of the Aeons), divine presence. Man has fullness (man in the great name)!"

The human expression is threefold. It is spiritual, psychic and material. To meet it is like meeting the divine. The Naassenes had an axiom: "The beginning of perfection is the Gnosis of man"

II

The golden man, this human pattern, man itself, is manifested in Christ, the Aeon Myriam's (Mary's) son.

The trinity in this human pattern announced the threefold word of the heavenly representative of the Lord. For this reason, this man created three churches: the spiritual, the psychic and the material. In each of these, Gnosis has a mysterious designation: The Elect, the Called and the Bound.

The Naassenes said they disseminated the teaching of James, the brother of the Lord, through the apostolic woman Mary. Their symbolic Adam carried all of fatherhood in him.

What did they believe regarding the soul? The soul was threefold, as man and the church. This trinity did not disturb its unity. One unit manifested in three. The soul is the origin of creation – it is really the origin of all living things. In itself it has the nourishing principle like a mortal soul. Rocks and minerals only develop through the soul, and the soul has a bond to all that exists, a desire, this dark need that initiates a quest and that spreads around.

Everything loves. Everything unites. Everything is in movement because of the glowing desire. Everything in heaven, on earth and under the earth. Everything is in love with the soul, and requires pregnant embraces in mysterious and cordial copulation.

III

It is the Greek Aphrodite who presses her naked chest against the mysterious Adonis, united in the foetus, as ideas and powers. The weakened Attis ties the unspeakable pleasure's private nature to the soul. Virgil has described this in an inspired verse: "*Mens agitat molem et magna se corpore miscet.*" The mixture of the soul and the world is either spiritual or temporal, and it transforms to become the great and eternal Androgynous (Male Female), the divine *Mas-femina*.

When Isis was in search of Osiris's genitalia, the feminine prototype was separated from the masculine. And the masculine prototype has water as its emblem, because water is fertilized and contains the genital sperm, the seed. Isis made seven journeys in her search, because the seven planets wandered in their seven ethereal spheres that include all. Isis fell and rose seven times.

The Scripture says: «The Saint shall fall seven times and rise again seven times.»

The Naassenes worshiped the image of the sexes. Lingam represented the torch of life, which sometimes was named Yaldabout and the world father.

They sang: "In his hands he holds a golden wand, devious, a beautiful sight that wakes the dead from their sleep." Herein, the dead means the inactive feminine power.

IV

Adam, the typical androgynous, mas-femina, has the ocean as his emblem, the abyss of actions, which rose from the waves, from the heavens to the most unexplored depths.

The ocean, which floats downwards, is an image of the lower emanations. The ocean rises towards the stars as its inhales and its chest rises, and is thus an image of the higher generation, the children from above.

Generations can be corrupted, while the higher is eternal. "That which is born by the flesh is carnal, but that which is born by the spirit is spiritual."

Three mysterious words were used in the initiation of the Naassenes. These were: *Caulacau, Saulasau, Zaesar.* The first was given to the higher Adam, the second to the earthly, and the third to the mystical Jordan.

Jordan is the river that divides. It is the river one must cross to die from the lower to the higher.

It is this water that Jesus turned into wine, where he transformed the temporal to the eternal, mortality to immortality. "O death, where is thy triumph? Grave, where is thy spear?"

V

It may look as if they have borrowed their initiations from the mysteries of Samothrace. Samothrace allegedly had the unfathomable mystery of the Adam-principles. The statues stood in the secret temples. It was two naked men who stood erect with their hands raised towards the stars.

The image showed their aspiration towards the higher generations. The two statues also showed Adam's type and the Adam of regeneration.

This is the earthly man purified and exalted, through his likeness to the divine pattern. This is how man becomes the holy Korybant:

"Lift ye everlasting ports, and the venerable King will come!"

The voice of emanations is the holy ladder Jacob saw in a dream when he was in the dry valley of Mesopotamia. Mesopotamia is that great river of generation, which emanates from the primordial prototype.

"O, how fearsome this place is (says the Scripture); it is indeed the house of God, the gates of heaven!" and the Lord Christ adds: "I am the way."

The theory of resurrection came from here. Man becomes God through regeneration. He dies through multiple generations, and lives anew through divine emanation. Only the perfect Gnostic comprehends this mystery.

VI

Because of this, the spirit still lingers in solitude, and the spirit is God.

Our worship is not bound to be performed "on the mountain, nor in Jerusalem", but in the spirit, where Adam-Eve dwells, who has thousands of names. There are thousands of lights shining as an eternal flame.

It is the Logos of love, which at the same time is science and love, and which reveals power. It is the root of thoughts and of Aeons. It includes all that can be comprehended and that which cannot be grasped, creation and infertility, years, months, days, hours. It is the undivided point. Its image is nahash (the serpent).

The hymns of the Naassenes pay tribute to this spirit, and one of the most beautiful is as follows:

The law of generations is primordial intelligence!
chaos came to be through its scattered seed
Brilliant souls rose up from Chaos.
The soul clothed in liquid against death and the waves of depression
Sometimes floats up in clarity.
Sometimes crying in the mud of the senses.
Sorrows and joys,
cry and believe.
Control and release.
Wanders in a labyrinth of forms.

But Christ says: Oh, look, my Father!
Look at the war of evil.
Man seeks to escape the merciless chaos.
But does not know how to cross it.
Send me to help mankind.
Descend to retrieve your seal.

Across the aeons.
Reveal all the mysteries.
Reveal the shape of God.
Teach the holy laws.
Teach Gnosis.

Jules Doinel

(*l'Initiation*, August 1892)

NIRVANA

To Papus

What is this noise?
The world is a dream;
life is a lightning
- Which sounds fall back?
The peace of the grave.
The hidden becomes clear.

The joy disappears,
pleasure becomes boredom.
Loved ones passes away
- truth remains.
The flight of time
leads to Nirvana!'

Buddha reveals
a new law.
The heart has settled down!
- Existence is a dream;
Let us flee from its lie.
OM! Mani Padme!

Jules Doinel (*l'Initiation*, June 1889)

AFTERWORD

After Jules Doinel's death the Gnostic church continued to develop. During one period, it took in elements from Eastern mysticism, which the church's teachers regarded as akin to that of Gnosticism, and Doinel's project of uniting Valentinianism and the teachings of Simon Magus, took a back seat.

With Jean-Baptiste Bricaud, the first division of the tradition happened. Bricaud changed the course, and set a new foundation for a new direction within the Gnostic church activities by introducing apostolic succession[30].

Along with the Episcopal lines back to the disciples of Jesus, there also occurred a change of liturgies.

From the simple form we find in Doinel's sacraments, we obtain Gnostic Catholic sacraments which also carry a wider framework of interpretation because of the symbolic richness in e.g. the form of the Catholic mass.

It is under the leadership of Bricaud that the Gnostic church expanded enormously. It was linked to several orders and took root in several European countries. To many Gnostics this was the formative period, which would get precedence for most of the Gnostic churches that were to be founded in the years that followed.

Bricaud also wrote in a magazine that he in no way was the successor of Doinel, and that his church, the *Église Gnostique Universelle*, was only three years old, and was in no way connected to the church of Doinel.

The flipside of this development also brought discussion the early Gnostics would probably have abandoned; of which lineages were the most authentic, which liturgy was right, who

---

30 The belief of an unbroken chain of bishops, extending back to one of Jesus' apostles.

would be able to invoke the most authentic Gnostic traditions, and who should be able to call themselves a Gnostic patriarch of a true tradition.

The sound of her voice still sounds. Far away from these meetings. Heard in the silence between the spoken word, and the Gnostic mystery is conveyed, in my opinion, in small chapels, from mentors who do not promote themselves as anything else than the voice of Man in a world of turmoil.

Thus do I end my story of Jules Doinel and the Gnostic restoration. And I put it back in the hands of men and women who continue to follow the voice of Ennoia, as through a mirror, darkly; or face to face.

MAIN REFERENCES

Bogaard, Milko: *Gnostic Church History I-III* (outdated online mms)

Geyraud, Pierre (1954): *Secrets & Rites Petites églises, religions nouvelles, sociétés secrétes de Paris*, Émile-Paul, Paris France.

Le Forestier, René (1990): *L'Occultisme en France aux XIXéme et XXéme siécles L'Église Gnostique*, Arche, Milano, Italia.

Koska, Jean (1895): *Lucifer demasqué*, Delhomme et Briguet, France.

Material from the central archives of Ordre Reaux Croix.

BOOKS BY KRYSTIANIA

Ødegaard, Rune: *Nøkkelen: Sethiansk gnostisisme i praksis*, 2009.

Svela, Ove Joachim: *Kabbalah: Vestens levende mysterietradisjon*, 2010.

Corpus Hermeticum, 2010, translated and introduced by Ødegaard, Rune.

Salomos Oder, 2011, translated and introduced by Ødegaard, Rune.

Ødegaard, Rune: *The Key: Sethian Gnosticism in the postmodern world*, 2011.

Ødegaard, Rune: *The Gate: Sethian Gnosticism in the postmodern world*, 2012.

Nykland, Sølvi: Noreas Bok: *Drømmer om døden og skapelse*, 2013.

de la Croix, Désir: *Martinistordenen Ordre Reaux Croix*, 2013.

Bodhidharma: *Veien er Zen: Bodhidharmas lære*, 2013, otranslated and introduced by Ødegaard, Rune.

Ødegaard, Rune: *Porten: Sethiansk gnostisisme i praksis*, 2013.

Evjen, Knut: *Teofobi: Den gudfryktiges åpenbaring*, 2013.

Hanshan: *Frostfjell: Zen-poesi fra fjellet,* 2013, translated and introduced by Ødegaard, Rune og Lindalen, Turi.

Moricario & Ødegaard, Rune: *The Cabinet: Sethian Gnosticism in the postmodern world,* 2014.

Shuben, Tensho; Shihyan Kuoan: *Oksegjeterens zen,* 2014, translated, introduced and commented by av Ødegaard, Rune.

Shuben, Tensho; Shihyan Kuoan: *Zen of the Ox Herder,* 2014, translated, introduced and commented by Ødegaard, Rune.

von Eckartshausen, Karl: *Skyen over helligdommen,* 2015, translated and introduced by Ødegaard, Rune.

Hongzhi: *Mester Hongzhis Veileder til praktisk zen,* 2015, translated and introduced by Ødegaard, Rune og Lindalen, Turi.

Crata Repoa, 2015, translated and introduced by av Ødegaard, Rune.

Wumen, Huikai: *Ingen-inngangen Wumenguan,* 2015 translated and introduced by Ødegaard, Rune.

Doinel, Jules; Ødegaard, Rune: *Eglise Gnostique Den første gnostiske kirkens historie, sakramenter og lære,* 2016.